CW00687124

RETAIL
SUCCESS
in an ONLINE WORLD

RETAIL
SUCCESS
in an ONLINE WORLD

How to Compete—and Win—
in the Amazon Era

ROB FISHMAN
Foreword by **David Mattson**

© 2019 Sandler Systems, Inc. All rights reserved.

Reproduction, modification, storage in a retrieval system or retransmission, in any form or by any means, electronic, mechanical, or otherwise, is strictly prohibited without the prior written permission of Sandler Systems, Inc.

S Sandler Training (with design), Sandler Training, Sandler, and Sandler Selling System are registered service marks of Sandler Systems, Inc.

Paperback: 978-0-578-51727-8

E-book: 978-0-578-51728-5

I dedicate this book to my father Arthur Fishman, a true entrepreneur who never failed to show me what was necessary for success in business and in life. I will never forget his lessons.

Contents

Acknowledgments

This book would not have been possible without the support, contributions, and insights of: my father Arthur Fishman; my mother Rosette Fishman Gerbosi; my loving and incredibly supportive wife Lisa Fishman; our sons Ben and Alex; my business partner and dear friend Rich Isaac; our amazingly talented team at Legend Development Services, the Sandler Training® office in Hauppauge, New York, as well as my Sandler® brothers and sisters from around the globe; David Mattson, whose leadership has been an inspiration to me for years; Yusuf Toropov; Laura Matthews; Jerry Dorris; Rachel Miller; Margaret Stevens Jacks; Désirée Pilachowski; Jennifer Willard; Alex Kirby; Michael Lichtenstein; Karyn Schoenbart, who helped put me on this wonderful path; the staff of Fishman Jewelers; and all of the many customers and clients whom I have served for so many years and who have taught me so much, with every interaction, about how to be a better version of myself. Finally, I must express my debt to a true visionary, David Sandler, for his timeless creations and principles.

Foreword

The retail landscape has, in recent years, been a scene of constant change—and not all of it welcome to stores facing increased competition from e-commerce giants like Amazon.com. Let's be honest: This sector has been evolving at an astonishingly rapid pace, and some of the shifts have been deeply disorienting to owners, managers, and employees of retail organizations who had grown used to transactional, low-information relationships with customers. Many of these retailers have now come to realize that not all the familiar retail models will survive. Accepting this much is a critical first step. Remaining within one's comfort zone is not a viable option in any economy, much less a dynamic one driven by technological change.

Although it is certainly a mistake to long for the days when consumers didn't have online reviews to check, couldn't get their groceries delivered directly to their home, and couldn't order things like toothpaste, toilet paper, and other commodities online, that's not the only mistake you can make in assessing the future of the retail sector. It is an equally serious mistake to assume that today's buyers will not pay a premium for a superior retail shopping experience when it comes to the products that matter most to them—the upscale purchases where guidance from the so-called "trusted advisor" can make all the difference.

Rob Fishman's book shows persuasively that consumers can, do, and will continue to search out such retail experiences. The book is a game-changer because it points retailers who are willing to move outside their personal and organizational comfort zones toward a future of great innovation, great relationships, and great promise. Using the groundbreaking work of David Sandler, the founder of our company, as its starting point, *Retail Success in an Online World* shows you exactly how to create mutually beneficial relationships with such buyers—and how to keep them coming back for more.

David Mattson
President/CEO, Sandler Training

Introduction:
The Ever-Changing
Retail Environment

Change is mandatory. Growth is optional.

The landscape of the retail business is rapidly changing. The age-old model of merchants serving customers in a traditional brick-and-mortar destination setting has been challenged and transformed. In addition to "big box" stores, many of which have dramatically expanded their product lines, there is ever-increasing competition for market share from digital media sources and online experiences. Now, more than ever, it seems that successful retailers have embraced a dual identity in their markets, including both local and regional, or even global, experiences.

Many retailers have discovered they need both an online presence and the opportunity to have human interaction—for one-on-one guidance, the ability to touch and sample merchandise, and the experience of buying in person. There are many excellent books out there on online marketing, social media, and selling over the internet, but few address the modern retail experience. And among those, none do so from the unique Sandler perspective—one that draws on the

work and legacy of the founder of the Sandler Selling System®
methodology, David Sandler. My goal for this book is to use
Sandler's work to shed some light on the essentials of success
in the human interaction side of the retail world—the part
that separates successful retail businesses from those that
struggle and fail to adapt. It comes down to the experience
delivered by the people on the front line, by the retail selling
professionals who actually meet and interact with customers.
I wrote this book for them, and for those who lead them.

With the blizzard of changes facing the independent
retail sales professional in the current wired environment—
whether that professional be someone on the front line, a
business owner, or an executive—I believe it is imperative to
start asking yourself the following questions:

- What makes your company different?
- Why would someone choose to shop with you instead
  of buying your product or service elsewhere—at a
  local competitor or online?
- How have you adapted to the way people compare,
  decide, and buy products today?
- What will prospective customers find when they do
  an online search on your store? What will the reviews
  say? How will you stack up against the competitors?
- How strong is your unique selling proposition?
- Does your sales process create an environment that
  makes it easy for people to buy? Does it make it easy

for you to deliver a "wow!" experience to both customers and prospects?

- What memorable things do you do to keep your-
selves at the top of the customer's mind, even after
they leave?
- How up-to-date is the physical environment of
your retail location? Does it keep customers coming
back and encourage them to send friends, relatives,
and acquaintances?
- How proactive are you when it comes to promoting
introductions to the friends, relatives, and acquaintances of your most loyal customers?

In my three decades of work in retail selling (mine has
been in the jewelry business), I have seen countless changes
in the sector. I have helped clients adapt to what might be
called the "post-Amazon" retail landscape. I have seen many
businesses that flourished in earlier years fail to adapt, and
I have watched as many once-dominant enterprises lose significant market share—or close their doors forever. My job
with this book is to keep your business from becoming one
of them.

Adapting effectively to the rapidly changing environment
in which a successful retail business now operates means
taking a far more proactive approach than what worked in
years past. Simply setting up a unique or an expansive product
line, designing some print ads, and launching a website or
social media presence isn't enough anymore. You must learn

to think differently about the processes by which customers show up in the first place and you qualify and close those customers. Most of the retail giants who have fallen failed for the simple reason that they didn't change their way of thinking. Specifically, they didn't set up and follow a clear selling process, which is essential to surviving and thriving in the current retail environment. You can do differently.

On a positive note, there are many retailers in today's market who are doing extremely well, despite outside pressures and challenges. What are their secrets to success? One thing that I have noticed is that these companies are committed to exceeding customer expectations, not just meeting them. The critical priority is improving the customer experience. You need a process in place for doing that.

From inventory tracking to customer retention management software, from computer aided design and modeling to online engagement with customers and prospective customers via interactive digital platforms like Yelp and Angie's List (where personal shopping experiences can be easily shared with the world), there are now a whole lot of different tools at buyers' and sellers' disposal. The real question is, how do you build these valuable tools into a repeatable process for your retail business—a process that exceeds customer expectations while making it as easy as possible for the consumer to do business with you? How do you create and maintain a physical environment that attracts customers, ensuring a positive experience they will want to share with those around them?

Many retailers have wholeheartedly embraced technological change while not paying attention to how technology is vital to running a successful enterprise, such as the customer experience and the development of a strong sales process and culture. These are essential issues, whether you're managing multiple stores or an individual, boutique-type enterprise. The crossroads of technology and its influence has created an opportunity for close evaluation of your strengths and weaknesses followed by careful reflection and a proactive plan to make changes necessary for success.

Opportunities for growth include the online shopping experience, social media, and websites providing feedback, endorsements, and recommendations from your customers and clients—happy and otherwise. How do you not only survive but thrive in this dynamic, constantly changing business environment? How do you compete with the online experience, which consistently promotes ease of use, simplicity, unconditional guarantees, and speedy delivery? How can you more effectively maintain, if not increase, your share of the market? How do you leverage your strengths and provide a customer experience that exceeds expectations?

One answer: By identifying a process that dramatically enhances the engagement and experience of your customer. This means doing more than learning a lot of cool new selling techniques (although I will certainly be sharing a lot of those with you).

It's time to take a top-down, comprehensive look at the entire retail selling process itself. It's more than just knowing what to say and when to say it. A successful sales process lies on a solid foundation of behavioral change, along with the right attitude, or success mindset, and also the willingness to hone your skills in the application of advanced retail-selling techniques. These concepts will be covered in depth in this book.

Remember: Change is mandatory. Growth is optional.

ONE

What Is Your Retail Sales Process?

N ow, more than ever, the strength of a repeatable retail selling process has become a key differentiator for those operating in a more competitive marketplace. You must constantly ask yourself these important questions:

- "Why would someone choose to do business with me or my retail business?"
- "What process will make the buying decision easier and more intuitive for prospective customers?"
- "How do I help them self-discover their need to buy without putting pressure on them to buy?"

As you ponder your own process, I want you to keep in mind that retail sales is a profession to be proud of. It exists to create great memories and experiences for the willing buyer or customer. Retail gives you the opportunity to share your valuable expertise to help guide people into making the best possible decisions and to make choices that they are excited about and comfortable with, by drawing emotion into the mix and creating positive experiences that are often shared with others. Last but not least, retail gives you the ability to earn money while helping others.

In other words, your retail sales process should help you have fun, improve people's lives, and make money. That's what I am about to share with you in this book.

Done properly, an effective retail sales process is simply this:

- An ongoing series of authentic real-time conversations in which the customer's expectations are consistently exceeded through a well-modeled, skillfully crafted series of consciously designed interactions that take into account basic operating principles of human behavior and psychology on both the buyer side and the seller side.

And here's what a retail sales process isn't:

- It's not a script you memorize. (See "authentic" above.)
- It's not something you improvise, either. (See "well-modeled interactions" above.)

- It's not high-pressure.
- It's not a default setting that connects to what was familiar or comfortable to you years ago.
- It's not based on win/lose thinking. (Instead, it focuses on mutually beneficial outcomes.)

Note that while some of what follows is applicable to virtually any retail setting, the bulk of what I will be sharing with you is relevant to upscale consumer purchases that take place in a traditional brick-and-mortar retail environment.

THE "WOW!" RETAIL EXPERIENCE

A friend of mine, Marcy, recently told me of a recent "wow!" retail sales experience. She was fortunate enough to be the customer. Naturally, I wanted to know all of the details that helped create this experience for her.

Marcy told me that she had been in the market for a hot tub. She had looked up several names of dealers and had proceeded to a particular store based on its convenient location and the positive online reviews it had received. For the entire time she was at this retail hot tub and spa outlet, she experienced no pressure whatsoever. Alexandra, the sales professional working with her at this store, answered Marcy's questions, learned about what she was interested in, asked pertinent questions about her lifestyle and background, and ultimately guided her to make the best possible decision based on what had been discussed. Marcy found her time with Alexandra to be easy and informative. She enjoyed herself and was excited when she finally made the purchase.

When I asked Marcy to tell me a little more about Alexandra, her newly crowned "favorite" salesperson, her reply to me was that she felt Alexandra was one of the best salespeople she had ever worked with. Out of curiosity, I asked if it would be OK for me to get Alexandra's contact information and call her myself. Marcy agreed.

I reached out. I wanted to get another sales professional's perspective on the retail selling environment and find out exactly what process had created this "wow!" experience for my friend. It was clear to me that Alexandra had a process, and I was curious about what it was.

From the 30,000-foot level, it was exactly the process I've already shared with you. It was:

- An ongoing series of authentic real-time conversations...
- ...in which Marcy's expectations were consistently exceeded...
- ...through a well-modeled, skillfully crafted series of consciously designed interactions...
- ...that took into account basic operating principles of human behavior and psychology.

Let's break down in more detail how Alexandra pulled this off.

In answer to my question, "What creates wonderful experiences for your customers?" here is what Alexandra had to share.

- **A welcoming attitude.** Alexandra's belief is that people who walk into her store, whether they believe themselves to be browsing, buying, or even looking for help, are to be treated like human beings at all times. I have compared this concept to welcoming a guest into your home. This is the feeling to be conveyed to anyone walking into your store or retail establishment.

- **Being competitive (in a good way).** Alexandra is proud of the fact that she is competitive by nature. She loves to win. This is what fuels her true desire to get out of bed every morning with a purpose.

- **Writing down goals.** Alexandra puts her goals into writing. Not just business goals, but goals for every part of her life, including financial, social, community, health and fitness, and so on. In my experience, this puts her in the elite as far as sales professionals go—I would estimate the top 3–5%. Yes, you read that correctly: 3–5%. Although some very successful individuals keep their goals in their head, Alexandra goes the extra mile by writing them down. Her motto is, "If you see it, you can achieve it."

- **Passion.** Alexandra is truly passionate about what she sells. When I asked her what she sold, expecting to hear about all of the hot tub models, shapes, sizes, and newest technology, she simply said: "I sell experiences and memories." This, to me, was a great answer. She's not just selling hot tubs. She's selling experiences and memories that happen to connect to hot tubs. Talk about an emotional connection with the buyer. This was one of the first things my friend noticed about Alexandra. Alexandra genuinely cares about the customer experience and the memories they create; she knows that the sale extends well beyond the transaction at the register. In addition to her passion about what she sells, Alexandra told me she is also very passionate about health and wellness and about family as well. She said that many of her customers purchased their models from her because they wanted to spend more time with their teenage children, engage in more relaxing conversation, leave their cell phones out of reach of the tub (for the benefit of both the people and their cell phones), and enjoy more much-needed quality time with their family members. Placing a premium on emotionally powerful issues like family, quality time, and wellness moves Alexandra's discussions away from a simple, one-dimensional conversation about who has the lowest price.

- **Curiosity.** Alexandra is committed to finding out what people need. She has truly mastered the art of asking great questions, which helps her help her customers. Being cared for by these insightful questions from Alexandra lowers a buyer's "defense walls" and causes them to open up and enjoy the experience.
- **Being approachable.** Alexandra befriends everyone

who walks into her store. Living the rule of "people buy from people they like," she prefers to make friends with her customers. At the same time, she does not seek approval or validation from prospects or customers.

- **Being interested.** Alexandra shows authentic interest in the people she talks to. She lives Stephen R. Covey's famous rule from his book, *The 7 Habits of Highly Effective People:* "Seek first to understand, then to be understood." This level of person-to-person interest goes a long way in creating differentiation from the competition.

- **Being OK with "no."** Alexandra knows she, her products, and the store she works for are not for everyone. She also knows not everyone is going to be qualified to be her customer. That is perfectly OK with her—and therein lies her success. She does not appear to be needy in any way. Although she would love to earn the business, she is not tied to this outcome emotionally. This eases any pressure a prospect might experience from other salespeople.

- **Following through effectively.** Alexandra is committed to professional follow up. Once a customer leaves the store, she always sends a handwritten note, thanking them for their interest. In that note, she always includes a reference to something she learned about them during the sales process, such as an upcoming anniversary or the name of a teenage child.

- **Asking for referrals.** After installation of a hot tub, once the customer has had the opportunity to enjoy the new purchase, Alexandra circles back and asks how things are going. She also asks if her customer knows anyone else who is in the market. Word-of-mouth recommendations to the customer's friends, associates, and relatives has led to many other referrals and additional business. Although this sounds like a great idea, it amazes me how many retail professionals don't actually ask for introductions and referrals.

A side note is in order here. Recently, I referred a friend who happened to be in the market for a hot tub to Alexandra. You can bet on the outcome: another new customer for Alexandra. Why? Because my friend Marcy had had a great experience with her. Every experience that exceeds a customer's experience pays compound interest.

What Is a Highly Effective Retail-Selling Professional?

The descriptions I just shared with you of what makes Alexandra so successful connect to some timeless success principles of retail selling. Alexandra is a professional. The following definition, I believe, summarizes the essence of highly effective retail sales professionals like her.

Highly effective retail sales professionals:

- Create and support the self-discovery process.

- Facilitate, with integrity, the uncovering of the prospect's needs and wants.
- Facilitate action on those needs and wants.

Let's take a closer look at the three elements of this definition.

Highly effective retail sales professionals create and support the self-discovery process. Buyers have to discover things for themselves. Unlike the traditional model, which is all about telling, the most effective selling occurs when buyers are encouraged to draw their own conclusions. High-pressure tactics simply are not effective. This self-discovery process is critical to professional selling, in the retail environment and everywhere else. To "create" and "support" self-discovery, the salesperson must foster an environment of mutual trust and openness. The absence of pressure and the salesperson's ability to ask effective questions are two critical factors that facilitate the self-discovery process. Recall that Alexandra never pressured my friend in any way.

Highly effective retail sales professionals facilitate, with integrity, the uncovering of the prospect's needs and wants. Alexandra focused on supporting discussions about family and wellness to uncover powerful emotional gaps between where a prospect really was and where they wanted to be in life. This stands in stark contrast to most discussions with retail customers. All too often, the customer walks in fixated on one or two things—price and availability, say— and leaves the store without ever having been engaged by the salesperson on an emotional level about what's working and what isn't working in their world.

Highly effective retail sales professionals facilitate action on those needs and wants. Alexandra applied zero pressure to my friend's buying experience. But when Marcy was ready to make a decision, Alexandra was there to guide her. Often, this is accomplished by means of a simple question, such as, "How would you like me to help?" or, "What would you like me to do now?"

OTHER BEST PRACTICES FOR RETAIL SALES PROFESSIONALS

Alexandra exemplified a number of other best practices that I have seen in highly effective retail sales professionals. These best practices are worth understanding before moving into the main section of the book. I've summarized them briefly below.

Have written goals in multiple areas. These include, but aren't limited to, sales goals; also include business, financial, personal, health and fitness, community, spiritual, and so on. Alexandra wrote her goals down. Have you written yours down? What, specifically, do you hope to accomplish in the coming three months? Six months? Twelve months?

Know and commit to the most important business goals. These include the building blocks of personal success: repeat business and referral business.

Create and follow a proactive plan. Highly effective retail sales professionals don't simply wait for the next customer to walk in the door. You will see many of these champions involved in local networking groups and joining smaller groups of like-minded professionals dedicated to helping each other with referrals. Many of them are also members of local boards and charities.

Have an overall positive outlook. Anyone in sales can tell you that it can be tough at times. This is a high-rejection business. Think-it-overs, stalls, get-back-to-yous—these are all part of the world of retail selling. Maintaining a mindset of opportunity is essential. Alexandra's outlook matched up with the classic formula SWSWSWSW: Some will. Some won't. So what? Stop whining! Consciously adopting this mindset and rejecting the pessimism best exemplified by the donkey Eeyore in A. A. Milne's classic children's book *Winnie-the-Pooh* is one of the distinctions that separates superior retail sales professionals from everyone else.

Take responsibility for outcomes. Highly effective retail sales professionals avoid the "blame game," the habit of identifying as many external factors as possible that might be inhibiting sales, foot traffic, or "yes" answers. (For instance: "It is very slow," or "The internet has taken a lot of business away.") These professionals are open to learning from each and every challenge they encounter; they adjust their retail selling process accordingly. The result is steady, incremental, and consistent improvement. Personal responsibility is one of the paths to selling mastery.

Cultivate self-confidence. Customers and prospects are

more drawn to a retail salesperson who exudes confidence, not arrogance, in order to provide the information necessary to help suit individual needs and wants. One aspect of self-confidence is product or trade knowledge; another is being conversant with store procedures, operations, and policies. Yet another is the certain knowledge that they do not need approval from their prospects and customers. Although it is nice to be liked, effective salespeople know that focusing too much on making friends can undercut the task at hand, which is to help the other person make a sound buying decision. Sales is not the place to get your emotional needs met.[*]

Consistently control emotions. Highly effective retail sales professionals maintain even-keeled interactions with customers, even the challenging ones. They know there will be challenging customers—they know not everyone is easy.

Recover quickly from rejection. Great retail salespeople are perfectly OK with a customer telling them, "No, thanks." Why? Because they are tied to the process of selling, not the outcome of an individual discussion. They also understand that not every prospect is qualified to be their customer. This understanding of a mutual process of qualifying takes the pressure out of each opportunity and replaces it with a relaxed exchange of information in order to see whether there is a fit. This places much less pressure on the customer (and the salesperson).

---

[*] Source: David Sandler.

Become comfortable with money. When it comes to money in the retail selling universe, there are two different ways that salespeople deal with it: technical and conceptual. "Technical" refers to the manner and process in which money is discussed. "Conceptual" refers to the salesperson's own internal money messages—messages that can come from childhood. These can tend to be early childhood messages of apparent scarcity, abundance, or the appropriateness of the topic itself that might have come from places such as dinner table conversation with parents. I will discuss this more in detail later in this book.

Proactively pursue new business through referrals. While retail selling may involve a brick-and-mortar destination, there is a new breed of retailer or retail sales professional who seeks to find both customers and referral sources outside of the store. They take advantage of marketing events and promotions, generating additional foot traffic. I believe this trait is vital. Ask yourself: How many referrals have you gotten recently? What is currently preventing you from getting the levels of introductions and referrals you would like?

Develop effective questioning and listening skills. Highly effective retail sales professionals possess mastery in how they pose questions and are constantly learning new things about their prospects and customers. They are present with their customers, learning as much as they can with limited distractions, giving the customer the (accurate) impression they are the most important person in the world at the moment. In short, the best salesperson is more customer focused than self-focused.

Create early bonding and rapport. Great retail salespeople are well-schooled in how to approach potential customers, breaking down any type of buyer defense wall. They understand the buyer's communication style, engaging them in a professional and friendly manner. Instead of a traditional ineffective greeting, such as, "Can I show you something?" or "Can I help you?" or "Is there something in particular you were looking for?" they simply greet with a warm "Hello" and proceed to engage about the customer first, creating comfort and the early stages of trust.[*]

Discover the real reason prospects and customers buy. The best retail sales professionals understand what motivates their buyer. How would the customer feel after investing in that new item or service? What would they expect to happen as a result of that investment? Great salespeople get buyers comfortable enough to share this kind of critical information. They set the stage for an experience that will exceed expectations. This can only be accomplished through expert rapport building and superior questioning skills. In addition, they also understand the personal journey of the buyer from a more emotional place, as opposed to a presentation of the product's features and benefits.

Get commitments from prospects and customers. With

---

[*] Whether they realize it or not, they are following a Sandler selling rule: People buy from people they like and who are like them.

each comfortable customer or prospect who the expert sales-person engages, truthful dialogue emerges. This leads to clear next steps and the lack of wishy-washy phrases (like, "Let me think about it") said to avoid giving any commitment.

Possess a strong desire for success. The best retail sales-people are tenacious. They are what I refer to as "climbers," not "campers." Consider two different types of mountain explorers. The climbers will ascend to the heights and ulti-mately to the summit. Campers are satisfied to pitch camp when things get challenging and stop before they reach the peak. In the world of retail selling, climbers are those who are willing to learn, who are unsatisfied with the status quo, and who always seek new ways to improve themselves. Climbers see every day as an opportunity to learn valuable lessons and push out of their own comfort zone by being proactive and growing with each customer-facing selling experience.

Have a strong sense of commitment. For highly effec-tive retail sales professionals, this means doing what they say they are going to do regardless of how they feel about it. Specifically, they are committed to growth, to success, and to learning as much as they possibly can about their product or service and their market. This creates an excellent experi-ence for their customers, who come to feel they have been dealing with an expert who is committed to helping them make a good decision. Those satisfied customers refer addi-tional customers based on their shopping experience, which is driven by the sales professional's personal commitment.

Consistently build a network and create customers for life. Highly effective retail sales professionals create positive buying experiences for their customers, leading to a wealth of proactive referrals and recommendations from family and friends. By exceeding their customer expectations, they create a "wow!" experience, making the shopping experience a common topic of discussion in their network. They routinely hear things like, "Alfonz and Seandra recommended I meet with you to talk about how you helped them. They speak very highly of you."

Always learn and improve. Highly effective retail sales professionals are their own lifetime project. As a result, they are open to receiving feedback from their peers and management on possibilities to improve their work with prospects and customers. I call them Retail Champions.

SUMMARY

Notice that, although the environment of retail selling and selling in general has changed over the past several years, these timeless principles, based on keeping the lines of communication open, are shared by Retail Champions everywhere. They remain unchanged. They are the roadmap to excellence in the noble, demanding, and exciting profession of retail selling. Now let's get started!

TWO

Good Enough or Excellent?

Here are two rules about exceeding expectations I believe every retail sales professional should follow:

Rule #1: The customer is always right.

Rule #2: If the customer is wrong, see Rule #1—while building trust sufficient to let them discover for themselves through your guidance that you might be able to help them make the best possible decision.

Don't forget the corollary, though:

Corollary to Rules #1 and #2: Not every prospect is qualified to be your customer.*

With all the technological and economic shifts that have led to significant change in the world of retailing, it's important to understand what really works—as well as what really doesn't—in the current selling environment. Surviving in this market means not just meeting but exceeding customer expectations. In this chapter, I'll discuss the often overlooked key to doing exactly this: nurturing.

Advancements in technology and the online buying experience have made it vital that you look at your own internal and external processes that affect your marketing, your branding, and your customer interactions. While my core belief is that retail will continue to change, I see massive opportunities for success for those willing to take a hard look at improving these critical aspects, leading to an even more successful retail operation. Although it's true that the industry is seeing some well-known and established stores close their doors, you can also see many organizations that are striving to improve, that are adapting to the changing marketplace and customer tastes as well as the technological changes, and that are thriving. What has remained constant

---

* Source: David Sandler.

as an element of success is direct, nurturing interaction with a customer or prospect who needs help.

Customers and prospects are facing a problem and need some support in finding a scenario or opportunity to solve that problem. This is one of the main reasons retail continues to be a part of the shopping landscape and can never be fully replaced with a mouse-click or a 100% online experience. People will always need allies, and they will always be receptive to working in person with those they like and who are like them.

Let's look at some clear proof that retail can actually survive and even thrive in the age of Amazon and other online retailers. Notice that all of these examples involve face-to-face, present-tense interactions with prospective buyers in a way that nurtures the relationship.

PHYSICAL ENVIRONMENT AND THE HUMAN TOUCH: A FORMULA FOR DIFFERENTIATION

Noticing recent trends in what is a very competitive retail environment, the classic auto showroom has become more of a spa atmosphere with the addition of more than the usual coffee and other refreshments. In a recent visit to one of these showrooms in our hometown, my wife was offered a free manicure!

Recently, I read an article about the legendary fine jewelry retailer, Tiffany and Co. With many people looking at the impending changes and challenges of the classic retail shop model, Tiffany and its team decided to build on both models, encompassing the theme of enhancing and exceeding customer expectations by having an in-store experience called the Blue Box Café, named after their famous blue boxes and jumping off on the idea that everyone should be able to have breakfast at Tiffany. Of course, the catchy idea is derived from the famed film starring Audrey Hepburn. You can literally have breakfast at Tiffany now—at a Tiffany-owned upscale café operating in the same building as the famous jewelry store—and lots of prospects are doing just that. Again, notice the emphasis on creative interaction with prospective buyers in the retail space.

Another example involves a necessary minor home repair I made recently. The job entailed a trip to my local hardware store, armed with questions and my wallet, ready to invest a little time, get some education, and get the job done. Although I could have gone to YouTube, studied some great videos, and perhaps learned all I could about the task at hand, I chose instead to ask the expert at the store. Why? I wanted a real, live interaction with a real, live human being who had more expertise than I did in the science of sealing and caulking a shower.

It was his expertise and customized guidance I was seeking—someone to point me in the right direction, some human interaction. That's something you can't get from a YouTube video. And, that's what I got. Problem solved. Happy customer. Guess where I buy my hardware goods now?

Here's another great example of nurturing human interaction and the power of the retail experience. Our son had recently gotten married. In preparation, my wife needed to purchase a dress for the occasion as mother of the groom. In our local market area, there are some major shopping malls with the big, well-known retailers as well as many specialized, boutique style shops in smaller, upscale shopping centers. I was a member of the search committee, along with one of my wife's close friends, in our trio's endeavor to find the perfect dress for the occasion.

After visiting a few stores, we happened to pass a well-known local boutique. Curious about what they might have to offer, we went inside. There we saw rack after rack of dresses. The sheer volume of choices was overwhelming. It was only after we were greeted and approached by Rosemarie that everything fell into place. Here are some words to describe our first impression of Rosemarie:

- Approachable
- Friendly
- Knowledgeable
- Candid
- Experienced

My wife really liked one particular dress at first. Rosemarie thought it wasn't quite right for her, but she expressed those opinions tactfully, in a way that allowed my wife to reach her own conclusions without jeopardizing any of the rapport that had been created. When Rosemarie suggested a different style of dress, my wife felt very comfortable and trusted her guidance. Rosemarie led us to the register, and we paid. Successful transaction, based on the personal touch of a real-time human interaction.

Want to create the kind of differentiation Rosemarie did? Good. Let's start by reading the following phrases, none of which Rosemarie used. Answer honestly. What is your gut reaction, as a consumer, when you encounter them?

- "Are you planning on buying this item today?"
- "What will it take to get you to buy?"
- "If I am able to get you a lower price, will you take it today?"
- "This sale won't last long. You should buy it while we have it in stock."
- "This is a very popular item. It is an excellent seller, and it's available right now."

If your reaction is like mine, you may think of the pressure that lies in these often-heard sentences. Simply put, these tend to be code words and expressions that boil down to one thing: Buy now! That's called the hard sell—and it doesn't work. It puts buyers under pressure.

The real question here is how an effective retail salesperson can have better conversations while reducing pressure.

With that question in mind, here's a concept that will take

all of the pressure off, help your prospect feel comfortable, and instantly distinguish you from the competition.

THE KEY TO NURTURING: FOLLOW THE BUYER'S PENDULUM

The key to a nurturing interaction is to let the customer sell and close themself. Stop trying so hard. Get out of the way of the sales process.

Using just a little bit of physics to demonstrate this concept, let's look at two of Isaac Newton's famous Laws of Motion.

Newton's First Law of Motion

- An object in motion tends to stay in motion; an object at rest tends to stay at rest.

Newton's Third Law of Motion

- For every action, there is an equal and opposite reaction

These laws, with very slight revisions, also happen to govern the world of retail selling.

- A prospect in motion tends to stay in motion; a prospect at rest tends to stay at rest.
- For every action by the retail salesperson, there is an equal and opposite reaction by the retail customer or prospect.

This concludes the physics lesson for today. Let's apply what we've learned to the reality of the selling process.

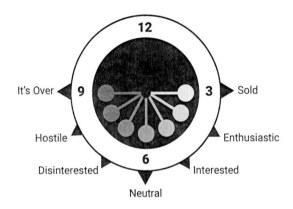

Look at the diagram above. It shows a clock face and a pendulum that represents the prospect's attitude toward buying from you. Assume the pendulum is at rest at 6:00. That means the prospect is neutral, not leaning one way or the other.

From that point, if the pendulum swings all the way up to 3:00, it's a sale. Commitment. Wallet and credit card in hand.

On the extreme other side, of course, is 9:00. Broadly speaking, that translates as "I am never, ever coming back to your store. Delete my name and contact information." They then join the witness protection program.

From this model, we can identify three general types of prospects/customers: positive, neutral, and negative. Consider 3:00, 4:00, and 5:00 to be positive prospects. We already know 6:00 is neutral. Consider 7:00, 8:00, and 9:00 to be negative.

Here are some of the comments you are likely to hear at each designated number:

3:00 "I'll take it!"

4:00 "This looks great," or "Everything we've heard makes sense."

5:00 "I'm interested in this model."

6:00 "Hi, I'm just looking," or "I'm going to think it over."

7:00 "I've been shopping at [competitor]," or "I'm not sure if this is the right item."

8:00 "Thanks for your time. I'll pass."

9:00 "You have some nerve asking for my business after the hassle I had here last time!"

Why am I telling you all this? Because there is a Newtonian* Selling Rule to consider here: Never get in between where the prospect is and where you want them to go. Considering the Law of Prospect Motion, it's clear that if you try to pull the prospect up to the 3:00 position, the natural reaction is for the pendulum to swing in the opposite direction. Translation: Pressuring the prospect always does more harm than good.

---

* Actually this rule was developed by David Sandler, but it sounds kind of cool to connect it to Newton.

7:00 Prospect: "I've been shopping at your competitor for a few years. They have a great selection of widgets and they are very nice people over there."

Retail Salesperson (trying to pull the prospect toward the 3:00 position): "We are so much better. Let me show you how great we are."

Or:

5:00 Prospect: "I'm thinking of buying a new car."

Retail Salesperson: "Great, we have some great deals. Let's see if we can get you into a new car today, OK?"

In each of these situations, the salesperson got in between where the prospect was and where the salesperson would like for them to go—which as we all know, is the 3:00 or "sold" position.

Watch the pendulum!

Let's take a deeper look at how to get out of the way of the prospect and allow their own momentum to take them to *yes*, without any pressure. Here's a possible exchange for each relevant number on the clock face.

3:00 Customer: "I'll take it."

Retail Salesperson: "Great choice. Would you like for us to gift-wrap it, or would you prefer to do it yourself?"

4:00 Customer: "This looks great."

Retail Salesperson: "I'm glad to hear that. Could you help me understand when you say, 'Looks great,' what that might mean?"

5:00 Customer: "I'm interested in [product]."

Retail Salesperson: "I would be happy to help you. Would it be OK if I asked you a few questions first to get a better understanding of what, specifically, you are looking for?"

6:00 Customer: "Hi, I'm just looking."

Retail Salesperson: "Of course. Welcome. I'll be nearby should you need any help."

7:00 Customer: "I'm not sure if this is the right item for her."

Retail Salesperson: "You know, I'm not sure either. Would it be OK if we take a step back and I could ask you a few questions to get a better sense of what you think she might like?"

8:00 Customer: "Thanks for your time. I'll pass."

Retail Salesperson: "I appreciate your letting me know. Before you leave, would you mind sharing with me what you were hoping to find when you first walked in?"

9:00 Customer: "You have some nerve asking for my business after the hassle I had here last time!"

Retail Salesperson: "It sounds like you've been upset with us. I apologize for what happened to you previously. It also sounds like no matter what we could possibly do, you would never want to come back, right?"

Notice that for each number on the pendulum, the conversation takes a position just behind where the prospect is, allowing them to feel no pressure from you. I am often asked which of these three general positions (positive, neutral, or negative) is the most difficult. The answer lies in Newton's theory. Both positive and negative prospects are already in motion, and are thus easiest to shift. The neutral prospect is the most challenging. Just think of how many times you have heard these words: "I'll think it over." No motion. Nothing happening. Nothing to discuss. The task here is to get the conversation moving. The only way to do that is by getting behind—not in front of—the prospect.

For instance:

Retail Salesperson to the "think it over" prospect: "No problem. I appreciate your letting me know. I'm curious. How much time do you need?"

If your prospect is willing to give a date and/or time to speak to you or to return, that just might be the path of a verbal commitment.

If, on the other hand, you hear wishy-washy words, like, "I'll be back," or "What are your hours?" or "I'll let you know," congratulations. You have an uncommitted prospect. This person may be, as the saying goes, blowing smoke.

Here is where the three most important words in sales come up: Nurture, nurture, nurture.

You can ask yourself a million questions: "Why are they not willing to commit to anything with me?" "Is there something I might have missed?" "Are they just not interested at all?" "Is it me? Did I do something to put them off?" "Is our product available somewhere else for less money?" Maybe it's any of these things, or a combination. The truth is you really do not know. So what you want to do is find out. If it is going to be a *no*, let's *know*. Nurturingly.

A possible dialogue with a neutral prospect might go like this:

Retail Salesperson: "Thanks so much for letting me know you need to think about it. In my experience there are usually two conversations that might occur when I hear people need time to process what was discussed. One might be, 'I need time. Let's plan on a conversation on a set date and time and get out our calendars.' The other might be that some people may not be interested at all and just want to be nice to me by saying they need to think it over. Could you help me with which conversation we might be looking at here?"

Customer (fessing up): "Well, to be honest with you, I saw this same item online and wanted to know if you are competitive."

Let's follow this dialogue through to the end. Notice that the salesperson never pressures the prospect to do anything.

Retail Salesperson: "I appreciate your letting me know. Would it be OK if I asked you a somewhat straight and direct question?"

Customer: "Sure."

Retail Salesperson: "It sounds like price is important to you. Is your decision to buy [product] going to be based on price and price only?"

Customer: "Price is important, but not the only factor."

Retail Salesperson: "So what might be the other factors involved?"

Customer: "Service is going to be a part of our decision as well."

Retail Salesperson: "Thanks for letting me know. I would agree that service is important. Where else have you shopped?"

Customer: "Online. I found a website that has this item for less money."

Retail Salesperson: "Got it. Makes sense. So when they told you about the quick turnaround in their service program, how did they describe how it works?"

Customer: "Actually, I don't know if they have such quick turnaround."

Retail Salesperson: "Oh. So, if they weren't to have such a quick turnaround time in service, that wouldn't affect your decision, would it?"

Customer: "So are you saying your turnaround for service is more efficient than the other?"

Awareness of the value you might offer has officially been created. This now leads you to a deeper conversation.

That dialogue shows you what it looks like when you get to what the neutral prospect is really thinking when they tell you they want to think it over. Can you see how much more can come out of such an exchange by using the pendulum?

This concept of the pendulum is a game changer for the customer experience. Take the time to learn, practice, and try to master these principles. First, get familiar with each clock face number; start envisioning what number your prospect may appear to sound like. From there, stay behind them in the number—always. "No pressure" is the theme, leading to a comfortable and enjoyable experience your customer will not only appreciate, but share with their own friends and family.

The mastery of retail selling lies in the way you handle these different types of prospects and the statements they make to you.

The Customer Experience Pendulum

Now let's add a different element to the retail selling experience and look at a new pendulum.

Consider, for the sake of argument, the customer experience that takes place after an initial sale. In this case, there is an entirely new and different pendulum you need to be aware of. Your customer has bought from you and might need some help with situations like the following:

- The item was a gift to a special person, but that person doesn't love it and would like to return for refund.
- The item was defective.
- The delivered item or service wasn't what was described.
- The item was found for a lower price elsewhere.
- The item is on sale now and the price was higher when it was purchased.

Have you ever faced these or similar scenarios? If you're like most of the retailers I work with, the answer is an instant "yes"—you have had to take care of the customer after the sale. Here is a variation on the pendulum you've just learned about that illustrates the difference between a satisfied/happy customer and the extreme opposite—the retail war zone.

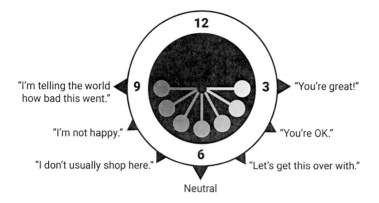

Here are some of the things you might hear at each point of the Customer Service Experience Pendulum:

3:00 Customer: "I appreciate everything you've done for me. Thank you!"

4:00 Customer: "This looks OK."

5:00 Customer: "I guess this is the best we can expect here."

6:00 Customer: "I was hoping you could help me with this exchange."

7:00 Customer: "I shop elsewhere. This isn't my kind of thing."

8:00 Customer: "I'm not really happy with what my husband selected. Would it be possible to return it?"

9:00 Customer: "I've had problems here in the past and I don't really want to do business here. I'm posting a bad review on Yelp/Facebook/wherever."

CUSTOMER SERVICE PENDULUM SCENARIOS

One of the things that makes retail selling distinctive is that the person at the counter must often be ready to perform flawlessly in two modes: sales and customer service. The two interconnect. In customer service mode, it is just as important to know how to get out of the way of the prospect, how to keep them satisfied and listened to, and how to allow their own pendulum to take them to an outcome that is amiable, respectful, and positive, without any pressure from your side.

3:00 Customer: "I appreciate everything you've done for me. Thank you!"

Retail Salesperson: "It's our pleasure! I'm really glad it all worked out. I look forward to seeing you at our customer appreciation event in May. You don't have any friends that might like to join you, would you?"

4:00 Customer: "This looks OK."

Retail Salesperson: "OK, good. I'm hoping you are happy with the outcome—is that the case now? I want to make sure you are happy."

5:00 Customer: "I guess this is the best we can expect here."

Retail Salesperson: "Thank you for sharing that. I really appreciate the opportunity to help you with this. What were you hoping I would be able to do for you?"

6:00 Customer: "I was hoping you could help me with this exchange."

Retail Salesperson: "I would be happy to. Have you shopped here before? I don't know if we've ever met."

7:00 Customer: "I shop elsewhere. This isn't my kind of thing."

Retail Salesperson: "Thanks for letting me know. Where do you typically shop? In your opinion, what is it that the other store does so well that it keeps you coming back?"

Or:

"So my guess is, you would not ever consider shopping in a similar store, even if there were new items, correct?"

Or:

"Let's pretend that I were to give you a promotional gift/coupon so you could experience us. Would you take it to get a sense of how we work with customers?"*

8:00 Customer: "I'm not really happy with what my husband selected. Would it be possible to return it?"

Retail Salesperson: "Of course. That would not be a problem at all. Can I ask you a few questions about

---

* Of course, the promotional gift/coupon you offer must be appropriate to the situation and the potential lifetime value of the customer.

what you did not like about this item and how I may be able to assist you?"

A side note is in order here: When you are in an "I want to return this" situation, you should consider yourself under an obligation to process the return, unless your company has a clearly stated policy that all sales are final and that there are no refunds. Even then, it is a good idea to process the return if it is possible to do so. Remember: We live in an era when a single "bad experience" at the counter can—and often does—turn into a social media storm in a given marketplace. You do not want to fight the customer. The question is, how can you help to move the relationship forward?*

9:00 Customer: "I've had problems here in the past and don't really want to do business here. I'm going to give you a bad review online."

Retail Salesperson: "It sounds like you've been upset with us. I apologize for what happened to you previously. It sounds like no matter what we might be able to do in the future, you wouldn't have any interest in ever working together again. Is that correct?"

---

* I strongly recommend a store policy of no cash refunds, but I must also note that too-strict and too-sudden adherence to "policy"—or even the mention of the word—is often an obstacle to delivering a positive customer experience. That said, I much prefer a standard under which customers receive exchanges when they wish to return purchases, so that they can continue to do business with the store and have a better experience somewhere down the line. If you have to set a policy, it should look like that. But don't call it a policy! And give your team some room to maneuver, so that they can work out constructive solutions to customer problems when they arise.

Notice how effective these responses are at continuing a constructive dialogue—which is really what you want to do in both the case of the sale and the case where there is a customer service issue. It is vital to watch the pendulum and never get in between where the customer is and where you want them to go.

Consider how the dialogue works (or doesn't) when these same words are handled with "typical" retail responses. Often, these conversations don't end well.

Typical responses (Is your team saying this?):

5:00 Customer: "I guess this is the best we can expect here."

Retail Salesperson: "Yes, it is."

6:00 Customer: "I was hoping you could help me with this exchange."

Retail Salesperson: "Do you have your receipt? No exchanges without one."

7:00 Customer: "I shop elsewhere. This isn't my kind of thing."

Retail Salesperson: "If you try this on, I will show you how we are better."

8:00 Customer: "I'm not really happy with what my husband selected. Would it be possible to return it?"

Retail Salesperson: "Store policy is no refunds."

9:00 Customer: "I've had problems here in the past

and don't really want to do business here. I'm going to give you a bad review online."

Retail Salesperson: "Sorry you feel that way. Lots of people do shop here."

As you can imagine, these exchanges typically don't end well for either the customer or the retail selling professional. There is only a downward spiral from here. The first 30 seconds of the exchange will determine whether the customer hurtles down that slope with you. Once you have initiated the downward motion, you can usually forget about creating a positive experience for the customer. You never get a second chance to create a good first impression.

Many people I work with are simply unaware of how badly their team is treating customers. Often, the poor service customers receive is the result of what I call the "leaky bucket syndrome." The service process has holes in it, because everyone is trying to make more sales. Sales are only good if they stick! If customers come back unhappy, you end up damaging your store's brand and losing market share.

Summary

Effective retail sales is not just about winning new customers; it's about understanding how important it is strategically to use a nurturing approach to hold onto your current customers—and get them to come back for more. Understand the magic of the pendulum; it can be a useful strategy for keeping both new and existing customers happy and comfortable. Never get in between where the prospect is and where you want them to go.

Nurturing really is your secret weapon. In the next chapter, I'll share some powerful real-world examples of nurturing in action in the retail environment.

THREE

Nurturing in Action

Years ago, a customer I'll call Xenia purchased a rather expensive necklace from our jewelry store on a Friday afternoon, then promptly returned it on the following Monday morning. Of course, we were disappointed to see this necklace returned to us and to be asked to give the money back to the customer. Upon closer inspection, we noticed the necklace had been worn—because there was an abundant smell of perfume all around it.

Unfortunately, there was nothing we could do. Had we placed a label on the necklace and made it clear to Xenia that if the label were removed, the item would no longer be fully refundable, we would have been justified in suggesting an exchange instead. But we didn't do that. Lesson learned. The customer wanted that refund, and she got it. It took us some time to get that perfume smell out of that necklace.

We had to do the right thing, even though this customer took advantage of us. Let's say instead that we did not give her a refund. What might have been the potential repercussions? The customer would likely never have bought from us again. Not only that—word would have gotten around. (As it happened, she had a lot of friends who were repeat customers of our store.) Not only that relationship, but many other relationships would have basically been over.

This may not seem like a story about nurturing, but it is. By giving the customer that refund, we kept the door open for future conversations. That's what nurturing is all about— keeping the door open.

A Good Customer, or a Nice Customer?

What is the difference between a good customer and a nice one?

A good customer is one who enjoys shopping with you, is a supporter of your brand, and recommends others to you. Even when things don't go well, they speak up and let you know how they feel.

A nice customer is one similar to the above, except when there is an issue or problem, you never know about it. They simply leave—and they don't come back.

When you keep the door open, when you nurture

relationships with customers and prospective customers, you make it easier for nice customers to become good customers.

My own journey in the business world has provided me with many real-world insights and lessons in the art of nurturing customers. Many of these were learned as the result of a bunch of mistakes, especially when it came to taking the first steps and following a clear sales process. After many lessons from the school of hard knocks, from Sandler Training, and from dozens and dozens of books and other sources, I have learned that an effective retail salesperson is best defined as follows.

Effective retail salesperson: Someone who nurtures a customer relationship with integrity, in a way that facilitates the exchange of ownership of a product or service based on the customer's wants and needs.

I would like to emphasize one concept: integrity. Integrity is the key to excellence in retail selling.

Notice, too, the words "based on the customer's wants and needs"—not your wants and needs as the seller, but theirs.

Seeing these words should give you pause. Those words should cause you to ask yourself, as I've had to ask myself many times: "Am I a self-focused salesperson or a customer-focused salesperson?"

Addressing this question directly was one of my first breakthrough moments as a salesperson, and I hope it's yours as well. Here's the breakthrough: It's not about you and me.

It's All About Them

Great selling, I believe, happens at the moment when your prospect repeats back to you, the salesperson, something you helped them to discover—something that they may not have been entirely aware of.

That's it: self-discovery.

Great selling is not convincing another person to buy.

How do you get to this point of causing the exchange of ownership? How can you accomplish that without being perceived as pushy or aggressive in the process? How can you move away from pressure toward discovery, away from trying to convince and manipulate people toward the goal of helping people make good decisions?

For some retail salespeople, that transition never takes place. For others, it is the journey of a lifetime. I wrote this book to help you complete that journey toward integrity sooner rather than later. I've seen what retail success and retail failure look like, firsthand, and I know how easy it is to slip into failure by embracing what's familiar. In this century, the traditional "it's always been done this way" mindset and belief is a recipe for retail disaster.

To reiterate: Change is mandatory. Growth is optional. Fortunately, growth is completely within our own control. It all begins with awareness and discovery.

Here's some personal history and context.

ALL IN THE FAMILY

My personal journey into the world of retail selling began in two separate yet eventually connected areas of my life. My first was growing up in the retail jewelry family business. As a child, I spent time watching my father and his business partner, my grandmother, demonstrate the art of nurturing relationships and creating trust, leading to great long-lasting customer connections. This had always been an essential ingredient, especially in New York's legendary diamond and jewelry district. There on 47th Street were hundreds of other retail jewelers on "the street" in what are commonly known as jewelry exchanges. You can bet trust is a key component of success in New York's jewelry district.

The retail jewelry customer would see booth after booth with a wide array of gemstones, diamonds, fashion jewelry, watches, and other items. Competition was (and I am sure still is) fierce. Every retail jeweler had both their neighbor as well as their competitor in the booth right next to them.

What was it that really created differentiation for my family? What was it that both my father and grandmother did that was so successful as they built the business? As a child, I recall watching them engage with customers, often laughing along with them as they would purchase unique and beautiful items in celebration of major life events such as weddings, anniversaries, and birthdays. I realized that my family wasn't just selling diamond rings, bracelets, earrings, pins, and similar items. They were also selling and celebrating feelings and emotions.

Even for the bargain shoppers, where price was their ultimate determining factor, my father had the ability to let the prospect know he could be helpful in making the right decision. People would let down their defenses and trust him completely. In this business, as with other types of retail models, there can be a lot of confusion about how to properly buy diamonds, jewelry, and other items of value. My dad let customers know they were always in expert hands with him.

Needless to say, my father had a profound impact on me throughout my life. When I began the process of writing this book, I had the chance to sit with him and ask him questions about his own experiences and what made him successful as a retail selling professional and small-business owner in the retail jewelry business. With my voice recorder on, we had several impromptu conversations in which he shared his philosophy about dealing with the public. Here is a transcription of what was, for retail sales professionals eager to master the art of nurturing relationships, perhaps the most important of conversations. Reading it now is difficult for me, as he has since passed on. I am grateful to be able to share it with you.

You can never judge a book by its cover [my dad told me]. In my store on 47th Street in New York, this couple walked in on a Saturday—an elderly couple, a tall fellow and his wife. I noticed her overcoat was very dirty and frayed and that on his, the button holes were all worn away. It looked as if he had had the coat for who knows how many years. He said, "You have a pin in the window that has diamonds, emeralds, and rubies in it. A flower. I would like to see it."

I looked at this man and said to myself, *I am going to give this man respect. Although he looks frayed and so poor that he can't afford this thing, he deserves that much. And who knows?* I took it out of the window, brought it in, and put it on a velvet display pad.

"Here it is," I said.

"May I touch it?"

"Of course!"

He picked it up and held it against his wife's coat. She had a hat that was at least ten seasons old, frayed and worn. He asked her, "Well, what do you think of it?"

She replied, "I think it's very beautiful."

He put it back onto the black velvet pad. He looked at me and asked, "Tell me, how much is this?"

Taking him seriously, I told him the price. I said, "It is $5,000. Do you like it?"

"Yes," he said. "We do. OK. We'll take it. How would you like to be paid?"

Concealing my surprise, I asked, "How would you like to pay for it?"

He said, "I will give you cash." He opened up his wallet and took out ten crisp $500 bills. He put them down on the counter and said, "Thank you so much."

I said, "Thank *you*."

While I was putting the pin into a box, he said, "Can I tell you something?"

"Sure," I replied.

"This is a little thing we do. I am a perfume manufacturer. I have a plant in New Jersey. Every weekend on Saturday, my wife and I come into New York City and to the jewelry district. We look to buy little trinkets. I went to several stores on the street today, looking at diamond pieces to get for her. We dress this way because we want to deal with people we feel want to deal with us. You're one of the few people who actually treated us with the respect we felt we should have."

He then put down his business card, revealing his name and position as the chief executive of his company. Then he said, "Anytime I can do something for you or your wife, please call me."

My father had described a "wow!" experience for both the customer and the retailer. It would have been easy to judge this husband and wife on their appearance alone. My father resisted the urge, creating a nurturing atmosphere and a judgment-free zone. His decision to share this story with me was a treasured learning moment I will never forget.

He shared many other stories from his years in the retail business that illustrate his understanding of people, his skill at discovering their reasons to buy, and his strategies for imparting the confidence needed to create long-lasting relationships with customers who would today be called "raving fans." I believe these combined to form his lifelong formula for creating repeat customers and generating referrals from their friends and family.

My father and grandmother were a great team. Eventually, my grandmother retired and the business expanded on Long Island, with my mother getting involved in running the new location. Watching Mother, I witnessed the very same nurturing principles in action: exceeding customer expectations during face-to-face encounters, holding in-store events such as cocktail receptions, and generally promoting a neighborhood feel. All of this led to countless introductions from friends of customers. This was not the standard retail model of placing goods on display and relying solely on people walking in the door. Often, our family was approached by local organizations and charities to contribute, whether through a cash donation or a gift. My mother and father took advantage of such opportunities because they knew that this consistent habit of nurturing relationships within the community helped build business in our local market area.

Years later, as I took over the helm, those guiding principles of nurturing customer care, learned through my family and shared with my own talented sales staff made the business a true success in our market area. I often run into past customers who will comment on a particular piece or design that I or my team had helped them with. It is a very gratifying feeling to have been able to help so many people celebrate life's milestones and special occasions for so many years.

My Journey

Today, as a sales development trainer and coach, I have had many conversations with retail sales professionals. I am always struck by how many ended up in this profession by accident.

I often ask my sales training clients how they ended up in this great and exciting profession called sales. A question asked would be, as a child growing up, what did my sales trainee actually say when their parents sat at the edge of their bed at the end of the day and asked what they really wanted to be when they grew up?

Astronaut? Police officer? Professional athlete? Actor? Musician?

Or salesperson?

Very few, if any, offered that last answer.

My own career path certainly did not develop in the way I originally thought it would. Like many other people, I ended up in sales by making a different career choice, too—and I am glad I ended up where I did.

My path led me to doing what I truly enjoy, which is helping those in sales and business development become the very best they can be through a healthy mindset, productive actions and behaviors, and the mastery of selling techniques. My happiness with where I have landed at this point in my life is rooted in my own understanding of where I have come from and the choices I have made throughout my professional career.

I suspect the same will be true in your case, so I'm going to share what that journey looked like for me, with the hope that you may be able to benefit from some of the experiences that ended up pointing me toward the selling profession— and specifically toward developing a retail selling process that included the key concepts of nurturing relationships and a genuine desire to help others.

Music has always been (and continues to be) a big part of my life. Growing up, I was into playing the drums and listening to many of the great rock bands of the 1970s. My earliest childhood memories were of my own aspirations to perform as a musician. Although both my mother and father were supportive of my dream of becoming a professional musician, they often had to tell me to lower the volume when I practiced my drumming in the basement growing up. Boy, they were patient and understanding.

At the age of sixteen, through a connection of my parents, I was introduced to the man who would become my long-time music mentor and teacher, Richard Horowitz. Dick was a percussionist and the principal timpanist with New York's Metropolitan Opera Orchestra. In talking to him, I realized how exciting the world of professional music was and how accomplished one could become. Dick was a talented performer who had passion for many aspects of the music profession. Aside from his performance mastery, he was in demand for his skill in creating handmade batons for many famous orchestra conductors. (Leonard Bernstein was a devotee of Dick's batons). Dick also possessed perfect pitch, the innate ability to recognize a particular note on the scale (which is a real blessing for a timpanist as there are usually note changes needed). It was my honor to study with him for many years.

I remember one afternoon, after a lesson, catching a ride downtown with him in his simple, yet very cool, early-1970s Volkswagen Beetle. I noticed that he never used the clutch to shift gears, which seemed impossible. Eventually I asked him how he could drive a standard transmission without using the clutch or damaging the car. Dick said he didn't need the clutch. He only needed to hear the pitch in the sound of the engine. The sound allowed him to identify the perfect moment to shift gears without depressing the clutch. Now that was impressive!

I learned a lot about people skills from Dick. In our weekly lessons in the lower levels of the Metropolitan Opera House, I remember how everyone seemed to know him and how engaging and friendly he was to anyone he happened to run into. I noticed that the close personal connections of the relationships Dick maintained were similar to the ones I observed with my father and grandmother in the jewelry exchange. They all had the skill of nurturing, the skill of making people feel acknowledged and comfortable. Not only that, they all had pretty good memories; they all seemed to be able to recall specific things about the people they came into contact with.

Dick was, in short, a master of rapport. This was evident in the way he was greeted by others at the Opera House, whether it was during rehearsals or performances. From the most famous people in the world of opera to the Met stagehands, people always seemed to be smiling when he was around. One of the great life lessons I learned from him was something he said to me often: "There's no substitute for experience." (He certainly had plenty of experience; he spent a total of 66 years with the Metropolitan Opera orchestra.)

This mantra was part of his worldview and part of the way he sustained his career. It has become part of my worldview and my career as well. To this day, I find myself saying these very same words to my sales training and coaching clients as well as orchestra members I work with when I am doing musical direction. You must make sure you get the experience you need—especially when it comes to nurturing prospective retail customers.

This means noticing the way in which you learn and adopt new techniques and strategies. Often these are mastered only through slow and methodical repetition until there is a degree of mastery of that specific task. I often refer to some of the music profession's greats, such as legendary violinist Itzhak Perlman and his method of practice. Repetition is a major part of his routine. It needs to be a major part of yours, too. That's something to bear in mind as you encounter the nurturing techniques I'll be sharing with you in later chapters of this book. You must practice them repeatedly, until they become second nature.

Sales and Music Overlap

Upon graduating from a music conservatory near New York City, I found that I had to engage my selling and nurturing skills in order to get work as a performer. This goal required networking—creating relationships with those who could refer me to others. It also required me to put myself out in the world in a way I hadn't yet.

It occurred to me that I could apply what I had learned about selling to supplement my income as I continued to perform. The path I chose was selling pianos and organs. It was in this job that that I learned just how different buyers are from each other and how I needed to change up my approach to each individual in order to create nurturing relationships based on rapport and trust, as I had seen my father and Dick do so consistently and effectively.

There were different groups of prospective customers. One group would only look at pianos. I quickly learned their key objective was to provide their children with the opportunity to learn basic music concepts and to apply traditional methods of piano playing, without any shortcuts. Another group of potential customers loved the simplicity of modern programmable organs, which bypassed the need for years or even decades of lessons in order to play a tune. It was clear these were two completely different types of customers with very different needs and outlooks. Yes, they were each pursuing the goal of playing music, but I soon learned that it was a huge mistake to treat the two groups as identical.

I began to customize my selling approach, based on which type I was talking to. Lesson learned: Not every customer has the same need or want. I realized I couldn't assume anything about what a given buyer wanted based on what I had heard from some previous buyer. In other words, I had no right to try to engage in mind reading. Years later, I would learn that David Sandler had formulated just such a selling rule: "No mind reading." Letting each of these types of customers tell me what they were looking for prior to my pitch made the process more effective. Who knew?

After several months of working in this retail environment, I found I really enjoyed the art of the sale. I loved getting to know my customers and their needs, wants, and individual tastes and preferences, and I got a real charge out of helping them discover the right choice for them. I loved everything that went into creating a positive customer experience (and the commission I got from selling a brand-new piano or organ).

As you can see, my personal career path as a professional salesperson emerged from a combination of life experiences and choices: hearing about, learning, observing, and ultimately running a retail jewelry business; studying music; and deciding to move into retail musical instrument sales.

Although my enjoyment of nurturing relationships, an integral part of the selling profession, has certainly been a constant, I will say this journey hasn't always been easy. Along the way I have practiced effective retail selling strategies with the same level of commitment that was necessary while I was practicing in the conservatory, and I have taken comfort many times from my mentor Dick Horowitz's wise words about practice: "There is no substitute for experience." Today, knowing how much he enjoyed what he did, I would add, "There is also no substitute for putting passion into what you do."

SUMMARY

Although the products and services I have sold have changed over the years in the business world, there have always been common elements and lessons. These key elements and basic principles have been and will remain timeless.

Great retail selling is the art of:

- Engagement with another human being.
- Nurturing the relationship by developing trust and openness.
- Asking great questions.
- Exceeding your customer's expectations.

Great retail selling is also the science of:

- Mastering a sales process.
- Developing a proactive business development plan.
- Getting to the truth by defusing distrust with disarming honesty.
- Tracking critical success metrics.

My job in this book is to help you master both the art and the science. Your job is to adapt to change effectively by changing the attitudes, behaviors, and skills you bring to the table.

FOUR

"How Long Have You Been in Sales?"

There's an old joke I've shared many times during training sessions with retail clients:

"So, how long have you been in retail sales?"

"I'm not sure."

"What do you mean, you're not sure?"

"Well, it's either been twenty years—or the same year, repeated twenty times."

If there's a question in your mind right now about how many years you've really been in retail sales, that's good. That means you're not an amateur. That means you're invested in growing and improving over time when it comes to mastering and expanding your nurturing skills.

Amateurs don't do that. They live the same year over and over again. They tend to immediately misfire upon the initial greeting or opening (if it happens at all) and plunge downward from there.

I am amazed at how many salespeople continue to sell this way. I have seen people hired for many retail tasks, including sales—but they've been given little or no training. Sales becomes basically an "also-ran" added onto the job. These people usually never want to improve their selling skills and proficiency. If you've made it this far in the book, I know you don't want to be one of them.

Perhaps you have heard one or more of these commonly used sentences by amateurs:

"Hi, can I help you?"

"Is there anything I could show you?"

"Do you need anything?"

"Did you want to see anything?"

Notice that these are all invitations to give a familiar, too-often-heard, two-word answer: "No, thanks." Variations include: "No, thanks; just looking," and "All set." No real questioning mastery here. Bottom line: No conversation. Which, to be fair, is an outcome the amateur is used to producing.

That's how it is with questions that are built around words such as *can, is, do, does, will, could,* and *should.* Technically they're called "closed-ended" questions, There may be a time and opportunity to use these types of questions. Professionals do not use them to open a conversation.

You may have found yourself giving the same "No, thanks" response to any salesperson who asks you a closed-ended question. Notice what happens when you do. The protective defense walls go up immediately between the retail salesperson and the buyer. You are locked down. Now, from this locked position of defensiveness, you will stay in lockdown, don't share, say-almost-nothing mode. You may even make a misleading statement or two. Who knows?

Although you may assume you know the reasons behind this defense, it makes sense to look closely at the motivations in play here. I believe customers raise this defensive posture to protect themselves from presumed manipulative behavior from the salesperson. This ties into a classic selling rule: "Buyers love to buy yet hate to be sold."* Food for thought.

Another example of amateur, one-year-of-experience-lived-twenty-times retail selling can be seen whenever you observe a pushy, highly assertive, and all-too-aggressive

---

* Source: David Sandler.

salesperson who sees one and only one potential outcome to a conversation with a prospect: They say all the right things and convince the customer to buy their stuff. This type of salesperson is everywhere. Take a moment to think more closely about what's happening in such exchanges.

The salesperson manipulates. They cajole. They bombard. No matter what the customer's reasons to buy, their approach is to say and do everything they can to convince the customer that their solution, product, or service has the best value, is the fastest, is the coolest, is the prettiest, is the most amazing. This is not so much a conversation as a situation in which customers find themselves standing in front of an open firehose.

These are amateur salespeople. But it's worth noting that they can be very creative in their approach, using all kinds of information about what they are selling and even asking plenty of rapid-fire questions to accomplish the all-important goal of closing the deal. Don't let the presence of questions fool you—no nurturing is taking place. Although this may be a memorable experience for the customer or prospect, it might not be the ideal memory you want the person to share with friends and family.

But isn't this what salespeople are supposed to do? Sell?

The answer is yes—but the process of selling has to be mutually engaging and mutually beneficial for both sides. The firehose approach fails that test. Even though it may sometimes produce a close, you have to ask if it will produce a glowing positive recommendation to family and friends.

Remember: A customer who has had an unpleasant buying experience, due to a pushy, inattentive, or otherwise nurturing-impaired salesperson, will tell far more people about that experience than someone who enjoyed a positive buying experience.

A few years back, in a local automobile showroom, my wife and I spent some time with an overly friendly salesperson Eric, who gave us a pitch and lots of information for a model we had been interested in. Feature. Benefit. Feature. Benefit. On and on he went. My interest in Eric waned the more he pitched us.

The discussion led to a series of obvious attempted closing statements, hints, and questions, leading to significant discomfort for both me and my wife. Pressure had begun to mount. Although the experience started out as a friendly exchange of "niceties" and basic information, it had now turned into a more confrontational experience, leaving us with the feeling of needing to protect our own best interests in the face of this firehose sales guy, who was now clearly on the hunt for another close—us. My wife and I started to physically pull back from him as he went for the close.

Although Eric was a nice enough guy, it had become more and more apparent to us that all he was really looking to do was get that car sold. We were another commission to him and nothing more. Our overall trust in him and in the dealership was plummeting. But the more we hesitated, the more he turned up the pressure. He said things like:

"It's a real beauty, isn't it?

"Lots of people are buying this model."

"Have you shopped around?"

"What would it take for you to take it today?"

"If we could come up with a good solution, would you be purchasing it today?"

He barely noticed our answers. Most of these questions were excuses for a soliloquy about the car's products and features. What was striking was how much he spoke about himself, the dealership, and the vehicle—and not much at all about us. Here's what we heard as he talked:

"I am going to demonstrate how well I know my stuff by reciting my demo and talking points."

"I am going to try to say anything that you want to hear—anything that will get you to buy."

"I am near my monthly quota. This sale will really help me."

"I will say just about anything that will convince you to hand me your credit card and move forward with your purchase from me. That's all I am focused on."

"I might even start with a higher price. Only if you ask me for a lower price will I start negotiating."

I remember thinking to myself, multiple times, that this was a textbook example of self-focused, as opposed to customer-focused selling. He didn't realize it, but the only reason we were sticking around was so that I could take mental notes on his terrible selling techniques. If you've ever wondered why buyers mislead and string salespeople along without making any real commitment, it is often a defense against an amateur salesperson's desire to separate the buyer from their hard-earned money.

I actually found myself uttering these words to salesperson Eric (and ultimately his manager, who continued the pressure when the sale was handed over to him): "We're going to think about it," and "We will get back to you." Yep. I lied. I got on the "Be-Back" Bus. This is a classic stall, of course, as is the phrase I used to decrease the social awkwardness by giving a false promise and the appearance of hope: "What are your store hours?" I used those stalls to get them both to back off and to relieve the pressure we were feeling.

We walked out of the dealership. We didn't come back. What happened? To get the best answer to that question, it helps to understand these basic rules of selling:

- People love to buy, yet hate to be sold.
- People buy from people they like and who make them feel comfortable.*

---

* Paraphrased from David Sandler.

My wife and I simply did not feel comfortable enough with Eric or his manager to buy from them. We reached a point where we didn't believe a single word that came out of their mouths. What would have made this situation more comfortable for us? How could the salesperson have built up credibility while bringing down our potential walls of defense?

Suppose he had made a better first impression with us. Suppose he had opened the relationship by saying things like:

Salesperson: "Thanks for coming in today. I'm Eric. And you are...? I look forward to learning more about you and how I might be able to help you with what you are looking for. Obviously, I would be happy to answer any questions you might have. Would you be OK if I asked you some questions to better understand what you are looking for?"

Us: "Sure."

Salesperson: "Great. So, where are you two from? Live locally?"

Us: "Oh, we're nearby. For many years."

Salesperson: "Good to hear. Thanks for dropping in and staying local. We appreciate it. So, can you tell me a little more about what you are driving now and more importantly, what you would like to know more about?"

On it would have gone from there—an easy and mutually comfortable conversation and sales process, with easy questions and easy answers along with disarming honesty added for good measure.

This is customer-focused selling in action: more comfort; more talking from the customer; more potential self-discovery versus being pressured. Nurturing.

Our experience with Eric might have ended up very differently had he moved away from the hard sell and manipulation and toward a more refined questioning strategy and an atmosphere of disarming honesty. To put it bluntly, his selling tactics just don't work. He was so used to using them that he simply couldn't see any other way to interact with prospective buyers. His high-pressure model of selling is dangerously out of date. It might have delivered marginal results a couple of decades ago—although even then it was a risky and inefficient way to make a living. Now, in the current retail environment, it's a recipe for irrelevance.

Again: twenty years in sales, or the same year, twenty times in a row?

Think of an amazing customer service experience you have had. Think of the last time you were in a store and you made a major purchase you felt great about, thanks to the other person's professional selling process and ability to nurture the emerging relationship. Now think of the last time a salesperson tried to manipulate, coerce, and convince you and left you feeling like you didn't enjoy the experience. These two different experiences boil down to whether the relationship was being nurtured. In the first instance, you felt comfortable, relaxed, and listened to; in the second, you felt on guard, defensive, and pressured.

Everyone has been there. Sometimes, you might have been interacting with a professional retail salesperson, someone who was always ready to help, suggest, and support you as you made the best possible decision. Sometimes, all the salesperson wanted to do was close the deal—with you or with anyone else who could fog a mirror.

Here's what I want you to bear in mind. Both scenarios are quite common. But, only one is more likely to be shared in person and online.

It is the negative experience customers are far more likely to remember and pass along within their own circle of friends and family. It's possible you yourself have registered more complaints about terrible interactions with retailers than shared stories about great service and great follow-through. That's just basic human nature. There may be an evolutionary component to it: humans may benefit collectively when members of the community share details of negative experiences. Whatever the cause, it's reality. People complain more than they praise.

"It takes twelve positive experiences to make up for one unresolved negative experience."
—*Ruby Newell-Legner,* Understanding Customers

Over the years, I recall hearing story after story of unpleasant experiences in car dealerships, retail clothing stores, upscale boutiques, larger department stores, you name it. People remember bad interactions and spread them around. This is why some businesses don't survive in this highly competitive market. They don't realize the enormous—and these days, often amplified—effects of even a single negative customer experience.

You are reading this book because you are willing to take your own game to the next level, to grow and improve over time in order to minimize or turn around any negative interactions and maximize the positive outcomes. That process begins with awareness.

_____

"Awareness is, itself, curative."
—*Fritz Purls*

_____

Let's examine more closely your potential retail selling gaps or challenges, no matter what level of expertise you might have. Start with completing this sentence:

As a retail selling professional, I could be more effective and sell more, if only I could...

Take a moment to write the answers down on a separate sheet of paper. Make sure you draw a vertical line down the middle of the page. On the left side, you will write things that are in your control (like the way you open conversations and your mental attitude). On the right side you will list those things not in your control (the economy, the weather, the stock market, and so on). Of course, you can fill in both columns, but it is a much better idea to focus on those issues that you can control.

Have you completed your list? Please don't continue with the book until you've done this.

Since you have no control over any items you may have placed on the right side of the page, let's not spend time trying to change them.

Instead, let's focus on the left side, on those things that you believe are in your control. Here are some of the most common responses I hear.

- As a retail selling professional, I could be more effective and sell more if only I could:

  * Get more people to focus less on price and more on the value I am trying to sell them.

  * Get people to let down their wall of defensiveness and trust me when I speak with them.

  * Have a more effective system of selling that would help me qualify or disqualify people, rather than spinning my wheels and wasting a lot of time.

  * Sell better against competitors including online retailers.

  * Learn to communicate better with people, leading to more open conversations with them.

- Do less telling and more selling—and stop talking too much.
- Deal more effectively with "We'll be back!" and similar responses.
- Figure out when people are really telling me the truth and when they might not be.
- Have a better way of closing sales.
- Do a better job of asking for referrals and endorsements from existing customers.
- Learn to not get frustrated from the rejection of a lost sale.

These are all common challenges for people in retail sales. These challenges come from two separate and equally important foundational issues: technical or conceptual.

Technical issues are basically the how and what of the selling process itself. These include the use of mastered and well-executed selling techniques and strategies that nurture the prospective buyer and promote a flow of comfort while uncovering information to better help the prospect make a decision they are happy and comfortable with. (Note that the car salesman who pressured us didn't have a viable process for putting us at ease or making us feel comfortable, which meant he didn't have a viable sales process.) I'll be focusing on these technical issues in depth in later chapters of this book.

Conceptual issues are all about what happens within the six inches of valuable space located between your left and right ears. Fear, doubt, worry, negativity, lack of confidence, arrogance, and a desire to stick with what's familiar (even when it's not working) are all possible obstacles. In other words, this is about your mindset and your belief system. (Note that the car salesman who pressured us was arrogant and was having real problems moving beyond what was familiar to him.) In the pages that follow, I'll be focusing on the conceptual side of selling as well.

Sales Malpractice

In the medical profession, prescription without diagnosis is malpractice. It's true in sales as well.

Think of your most recent visit to your physician. Regardless of whether it was an annual physical or a health-related issue, it is highly probable you were asked many questions. Stop and think about all the questions doctors have asked you. What do you think the total number might be? 35? 50? 100? More?

Why so many questions? It's obvious. A doctor is a professional who would not render a diagnosis without gathering the needed information.

Now, if you apply this same principle to the world of retail selling, you can begin to notice just how many salespeople commit sales malpractice every working day. They don't ask many questions, so there's not much discovery of the prospect's true needs and wants. They make assumptions with zero nurturing.

In many if not all of the ineffective sales experiences

consumers have, the salesperson is eager to write out a prescription (the pitch or presentation) without having conducted any kind of diagnosis (questioning strategy).

Again, I'd like you to think of a recent interaction involving a potential major purchase with a retail selling professional. Here are some questions for you to consider:

- Was this salesperson avoiding opportunities to actually listen to you?
- Did they seem to care only about making that sale?
- Did you have the feeling of being manipulated, that your own best interests as the buyer were not being served?
- Did you find it difficult to trust this salesperson?
- Did you avoid opening up and discussing your issues/desires/wants freely?
- Was this salesperson pushy and aggressive?
- Did they talk way too much?
- Was this salesperson focused too much on themself?

As you examine your own answers to these questions one thing becomes clear. Sales malpractice does not work. In fact, it backfires—sometimes quite spectacularly. It only generates negative chatter among prospective buyers that you simply can't afford in this era of instant feedback on public social platforms. Ouch!

The good news is that there are tested, proven, and effective strategies and tactics that can and will help you move away from the sales malpractice model. All you need are the technical and conceptual best practices I'll be sharing with you—best practices that have been shown to improve every aspect of the retail sales process.

Summary

This book gives you the tools you need to develop awareness and create an environment of mutual trust and respect. Yes, there really are specific behaviors and beliefs that help salespeople create authentic mutual trust and understanding in the selling process. As the prior chapters have shown, the traditional retail world and its selling model is undergoing a period of tremendous change. Those who survive (and ultimately thrive) in the retail sector will be those who commit to developing themselves professionally and adapting to an ever-changing environment.

The first step in this comprehensive process of improvement and adaptation is the willingness to self-assess. That's what you'll begin to take on in the next chapter.

FIVE

Choose Your Zone

Human beings generally operate in one of two zones: a growth zone or a comfort zone. Which do you prefer? The choice is yours.

In retail sales, there is an abundance of people in the zone of comfort. That may sound at first like a good thing, but consider that psychologists describe this space as follows:

Comfort zone: an environment or situation in which a person feels secure or at ease; any routine in which a person feels comfortable as long as there is no drastic change.

In my work with individual sales professionals, their teams, and their leadership, I typically begin my training and coaching by showing participants a model depicting four different zones. I ask them where they see themselves.

At the top of these four zones sits the Success Triangle[*] (which I will cover in detail in the next chapter). Connected to the triangle is the growth zone, which is the pathway to achieving success. Below the growth zone is the panic zone

---

*   Source: Sandler Selling System.

(about which more in a moment) and the comfort zone, a heavily trafficked area that is home to many who have done well and have had a reasonable amount of success. These people tend to take their foot off the gas pedal and settle for coasting a little. After all, with a recent win, they may decide to not work as hard and to chill out.

The panic zone is what occurs when either the salesperson or the company is in growth zone while the other stays in the comfort zone. I have seen this occur both ways. The company has lost a few (or maybe more than a few) excellent retail selling professionals as store management has remained stagnant, unwilling to adapt to the changing marketplace or they are in a comfort zone. They aren't treating the sales team with mutual respect or even giving them growth opportunities or holding them accountable. Personal and professional development is not a part of the company culture, leading to the mindset of playing it safe, merely not losing.

Compare this to the culture of winning. When a salesperson enters the panic zone, this is primarily due to the company making changes in the way it does business, approaches the market or its customers, compensates the team, and so on. This sometimes leads to a salesperson in the comfort zone deciding it is time to get their act together, as things seem to be changing. In both cases, people realize that things have to change.

The dead zone is the result of the resistance to moving into the comfort zone, minus any real efforts at improvement. The dead zone is often the end of the road for the individual or, in some cases, for the company itself. There are countless examples nowadays of companies that have exited the retail landscape due to their own addiction to the comfort zone. If strategies or tactics are brought, they are acted on only when it's too late. The same can often be said about the sales teams these companies hold onto. Companies that continue to hire and retain mediocre salespeople tend to find themselves bleeding precious market share. It's a sad reality.

"Change is mandatory. Growth is optional."
—John C. Maxwell

So, which zone is for you? Here are some distinctions that will help you map out which of these two areas you want to function in:

- **Comfort zone:** Old stories, old games, old conclusions, and no new processes or ideas. Everything's very familiar. When something goes wrong, it's someone else's fault—not yours. Beliefs in the comfort zone can tend to be limited. This is known as self-limiting head trash, or to use a better definition, the things a person believes to be true even though there actually may not be a shred of evidence to prove it.

- **Growth zone:** You are learning from failure and using it as an event to grow, develop, and improve. You are accountable. You are resilient, tenacious, willing to take risks, and eager to learn the brutal facts and truths in order to have consistent improvement. You are asking more gutsy questions of prospects and customers. You have learned to not take failure or rejection personally.

To that last point: When a customer or prospect says, "No, thank you," or "I'm not interested," is it a rejection of you as a human being or the role of the sales professional, the role that you have signed up for? There is an art to failure. Mastering it lies in the mindset of the person in question. If that person is operating within the growth zone, then failure is merely an event and not a judgment on the person.

People in the growth zone are tenacious. They bounce back because they understand that failure is not about them as a person. They learn from each experience; they are willing to confront the facts and make the necessary changes to improve themselves. They see themselves as always developing and improving. Although they possess a clear vision and set aggressive goals for themselves, they tend to enjoy the journey and find their work rewarding, even when adversity strikes. Their mindset sounds like this:

- "I am constantly learning and enjoy the process of development." These people never stop growing and learning.
- "I am tied to the sales process, not the outcome." This is an indicator of a growth-minded individual who

finds true success is developing and using a system in selling.

- "I am open to feedback from those in management on how to be better and better each and every day." If there is a problem, these people want to know about it. They are all about reality.

This reality focus is extremely important. A sense of awareness about where positive change needs to happen sets in, creating a gap between what is happening now and what needs to happen, and also the energy to take action for those who see the gap and are willing and able to confront it. This begins the process of growth, which can also be seen as the opposite of discomfort (one of the key ingredients to real growth). It happens through experiencing that gap or, as it is also called, pain.

There is no growth without pain.

Here is what the comfort zone sounds like:

- "I've been doing this for many years now, and I don't need to change anything."
- "Things are relatively good. I'm satisfied with where things are right now."
- "I just closed a nice sale. Time to take a break for a little while."

- "I know what I am doing. No need to learn anything new."
- "It's the same old thing."

"Good enough" is the mindset of the person in the comfort zone.

The panic zone can be seen as the intermediate result of the gap created by the difference between comfort and growth within the individual. In the case of the retail selling professional moving into the panic zone, it may happen to them as a result of learning new products, services, policies, or warranties that the organization is putting in place to keep market share. That salesperson may try to stay in the comfort zone at first, only to come to the realization that they may be at risk by not openly embracing the change and seeking constant improvement or change. This is the panic zone.

You will typically see high turnover in the sales department when the organization is in the panic zone. Other symptoms are: management is not keeping up with strategies to maintain market share; not enough training is provided to create a competitive edge in a rapidly changing environment; and there isn't a suitable process for hiring, recruiting, and onboarding new retail salespeople. Additionally, management starts to view sales as an afterthought or even as an additional function of a job that handles other tasks, such as inventory, retail floor merchandising, in-store promotions, or customer service. Very often, this leads to high turnover in good retail salespeople. These talented, growth-oriented people prefer to work in a company that shares the same vision of success and knows that it happens through constant feedback, training, and development. In other words, the growth zone.

As a result, many retail customers of companies in the panic zone will encounter a mediocre salesperson. Although they may be friendly, that friendliness might consist of a brief conversation, some initial discovery of needs, a nod, some basic facts, maybe a smile—a mediocre experience at best. They might even ask the customer to buy. The customer may even make that purchase anyway. A potential result is that this customer won't recommend this less-than-ideal salesperson to family and friends—and won't return to you as a resource.

SUMMARY

The true path to success is through the growth zone. Traveling this path requires a personal understanding of the differences between this zone and the comfort, panic, and dead zones.

The Success Triangle, discussed in detail in the following chapter, will give you a powerful daily blueprint for success in retail selling. It lies in the growth zone.

Remember: Change is mandatory. Growth is optional.

SIX

The Success Triangle

S uccess in retail sales (and, for that matter, in all other aspects of life) can be illustrated with the Success Triangle (shown on the next page). Think of this as your personal roadmap for success. This roadmap covers three elements: attitude, behavior, and technique. Let's break down each of these now.

ATTITUDE

The previous chapter discussed the four different zones of performance. Much of the difference between those zones lies in the mindset of success—in the internal messaging that occurs in the six inches between the ears.

The effective retail sales professional possesses an overall healthy mindset. That means they are able to deal with rejection whenever it happens—and it sure does in selling. It also means they are able to control and, ultimately, master their emotions, consistently keeping a degree of professionalism in all their interactions.

Retail salespeople who have mastered the attitude corner of the triangle have a core belief in themselves, their company and the market they serve. Other words to describe this point on the triangle include mindset, belief, and conviction. Accomplished retail sales professionals maintain their composure and reflect confidence even during challenging conversations with prospects regarding price and in other negotiation settings.

Their internal belief is that they are there to help their customer in the process of mutual help through discovery and to create an experience that is aimed to not only meet but exceed the expectations of their clientele. If there isn't a fit between them, the salesperson is comfortable with the "no, thanks" response because it leads to shaking hands and parting as friends. They don't take it personally. They realize they may not be for everyone, and they don't let their emotions get the best of them. They are in pursuit of the truth in an environment of absolute professionalism. What makes these people so special is their focus on the loyalty created by helping these customers, even if it means sending them elsewhere for that single purchase.

BEHAVIOR

Ready for a surprise? It's not how you feel that determines how you act. It's how you act that determines how you feel.

This rule relates to the behavior corner of the triangle. It's all about doing what you commit to doing, regardless of how you may feel at the moment. In my work with retail business owners with their sales teams, I often see that retail salespeople tend to be more reactive than proactive about building their customer or client base. Most retail salespeople do not set long-term or short-term goals for themselves. They typically live in the day-to-day grind without a plan in place. Same old, same old. After all, it's the way retail has always been done, right? Sounds like the comfort zone, doesn't it?

The truly successful retail selling professional is proactive at engaging in activities outside the walls of their retail establishment. Often, they join local networking groups, professional or business associations, and boards of charities in order to build a solid referral base with strategic partners and prospective customers. Even though networking has not been traditionally associated with retail selling, it is now emerging as an important, and indeed essential, competitive advantage.

A classic example of a referral partner from the world of traditional sales would be the residential real estate agent or broker who creates a strategic relationship with a local banker or mortgage professional. In the retail world, this kind of alliance might be a high-end automobile dealer and a strategic relationship with an insurance agent who specializes in property and casualty insurance. Since they are not competitors, these professionals can actually create long-lasting relationships with each other, knowing, with the creation of this new relationship, they now possess a resource for mutual introductions and new business opportunities leading to increased store traffic and better quality leads for both.

Generating introductions can occur through a proactive

client development and referral plan, via networking, that clearly encourages long-lasting relationships for mutual gain. The traditional habit of waiting for customers to walk in the door as the only source of opportunity will no longer do. Change the behavior. Go out and get it.

Other successful retail salespeople create loyalty by offering rewards to their customers, leading to an even more memorable shopping experience. They do this consistently with each and every new customer. Does this mean looking closely at your business model and at the lifetime value of a given customer? Yes! Is it better than a behavior plan that consists entirely of waiting for people to walk through the door? Again, the answer is yes!

TECHNIQUE

Time for some tough questions. When you open your mouth to speak with potential customers, do you sound like the typical predictable salesperson? Are you talking too much, not appearing genuine, trying your best to make that sale instead of asking effective questions? Are you repeating certain phrases simply because they are familiar to you? Is your motive to do everything you can to get the buyer to spend, even if that means creating a lot of pressure? Do you sound like you simply don't care enough to nurture the relationship or are too busy to do so?

Or, do you initially engage with the customer in a disarmingly honest way, letting them know up front that your job is a genuine understanding of that customer's needs? That your goal is to create a new relationship, build trust, and create loyalty?

The mastery and usage of effective sales techniques is designed only to create a warm, friendly, and, most importantly, efficient way of helping customers discover for themselves whether it makes sense to buy from you. This is a paradigm shift. It's one of the key ways retail establishments can distinguish themselves from the competition and increase the effectiveness and success of the physical selling environment.

"If the competition is doing it, stop doing it right away."
—*David Sandler*

THE COMPETENCIES

That, then, is the Success Triangle. Let's use it now to look deeper into what creates true mastery in the retail selling process.

Here is a list, based on what you read in Chapter 1, that identifies the core competencies creating true excellence in retail selling. Next to each competency, you will notice that I have flagged where that specific competency lies on the Success Triangle. Let me challenge you, as you read this list, to keep score. Be ruthlessly honest with yourself. Identify just how effective you are in each of these specific areas. Zero means you currently have no proven ability to execute in this area. One means you have some proven ability in this area. Two means you have proven mastery in this area. Three means you not only have proven mastery in this area, but you have also taught/coached someone else to do it.

1. I have written goals in multiple areas of my life (social, family, financial, community, etc.). (Behavior)

0   1   2   3

2. I know and commit myself to the most important strategic goals of retail salespeople. (Behavior)

0   1   2   3

3. I create and follow a proactive customer development and loyalty plan. (Behavior)

0   1   2   3

4. I have an overall positive outlook. (Attitude)

0   1   2   3

5. I take responsibility for my actions. (Attitude, driven by Behavior)

0   1   2   3

6. I learn all I can about my products and services and those of my competitors. (Behavior)

0   1   2   3

7. I am self-confident. (Attitude)

0   1   2   3

8. I consistently control my emotions. (Attitude)

0   1   2   3

9. I don't have a high need for approval. (Attitude)

0   1   2   3

10. I recover from rejection. (Attitude)

0   1   2   3

11. I am comfortable with money and its concept. (Attitude)

0   1   2   3

12. I proactively pursue new business through introductions and referrals. (Behavior)

0   1   2   3

13. I possess effective questioning and listening skills. (Technique)

0   1   2   3

14. I am good at creating early bonding and rapport with people. (Technique)

0   1   2   3

15. I discover the real reason why prospects and customers buy. (Technique)

0   1   2   3

16. I ask for and get commitments from my prospects
and customers. (Technique)

0   1   2   3

17. I possess a strong desire for success. (Attitude)

0   1   2   3

18. I have a strong sense of commitment. (Behavior)

0   1   2   3

19. I consistently build a network and create customers
for life. (Behavior)

0   1   2   3

20. I am always learning and improving the way I sell.
(Behavior)

0   1   2   3

SUMMARY

There are three corners on the Success Triangle: attitude, behavior, and technique. Understanding areas of strength as well as areas of potential improvement in each of these areas is the starting point of a growth-oriented career. Use the assessment that appears in this chapter to determine where you stand in all three areas.

SEVEN

First Impressions Matter

This book has talked a lot about changing the dynamic of the first few seconds of your interaction with the prospective retail buyer. Typically, this is the first and perhaps most important instance of moving beyond your comfort zone in the retail selling environment. If you'd like a glimpse of what's possible for you and your store once that comfort zone has been breached, consider the following true story.

A 25% Increase in Closing Ratios

Michael Lichtenstein is owner and principal designer of the Lighting Gallery, a Long Island-based lighting and home decor showroom. He reached out to me for help in adjusting to a major shift in his market.

"For most of our history," Lichtenstein recalls, "dating back to our founding in the mid-1970s, we were highly dependent on in-store traffic from individual homeowners. I'd say we derived 80–90% of our business from that group: people who would walk into the store looking to upgrade the lighting in their own living environment." Then, five to six years ago, everything changed.

"The whole walk-in picture changed with the rise of the Internet as a purchasing platform," Lichtenstein notes. "Whereas before we had individual homeowners who were our primary target market, now that market was increasingly driven by price alone and by online searches. Being the cheapest player was not the game we wanted to play. So we decided to alter our target to reflect the value we added. In our marketing, we began targeting individuals and designers and architects who valued customer service and knowledge—as well as a competitive price."

But there was a problem. Lichtenstein's staff members were still interacting with prospective customers like it was 1999.

"The old way of talking to people wasn't working," he remembers. "We needed to have deeper conversations with the people who came into the store about the design issues they were having problems with, and that just wasn't happening. Our people were defaulting to conversational openings that instantly caused people to shut down—by asking things like, 'Hi, can I help you?'"

That well-worn retail conversational opening caused prospects to disengage using an automatic, preprogrammed response. Not only that, it made customers less likely to share what was on their minds.

"The problem is, 'Can I help you?' is a yes or no question," Lichtenstein observes, "and it's just way too easy for people to bring up the defense shields and say, 'No, thanks, just looking.' Then it's much, much harder to support a more meaningful conversation about what problem they're trying to solve. People were coming into the store to get prices and get product information, and then they were leaving. That whole dynamic had to change."

It did. "With sales training, we got our team not just to begin the conversation differently, by opening the conversation with questions like, 'Hi, what brought you in here today?' but also to think differently about the discussions they were having with customers. The team changed their headspace, and we broke the pattern of thinking that everybody just wanted a deal and that the only way to close a sale was to give away margin. That's a subordinate position. Our people started working from the assumption that they had expertise in lighting and design. That's why people came to see us—to work with us on their projects and for us to contribute that expertise as a peer."

Instead of volunteering to get beaten up on price, Lichtenstein's team started assuming that they had something valuable to contribute to the conversation. They disengaged from low-value prospects and identified areas where customers were concerned about making an expensive mistake and were looking for help. This shift in conversational focus, an essential part of an effective qualifying process, created dramatic positive results.

"Since we started with the new selling system," Lichtenstein notes, "our closing rate in face-to-face interactions with prospective customers has risen by 25%, and the deals we are closing are larger. We're doing a better job of qualifying, we're disengaging from people who were just going to buy online anyway, and we're focused on adding value to the people who really are looking for a design partner for their lighting."

EIGHT SECONDS

Eight seconds sets the course. Eight seconds determines whether you are beginning an effective retail sales process or following the path of least resistance—which in today's market environment is the pathway to oblivion for retailers.

Eight seconds is all you have to either establish credibility and create a nurturing relationship with an engaged prospect or sow the seeds of mistrust, confusion, and doubt.

Here's eight seconds of retail disaster from yet another car dealership my wife and I visited:

Car Salesperson: "Hi, I'm Bob. What can I do for you?"

Me [pointing]: "I am looking for a new car and was interested in learning more about this model."

Car Salesperson: "OK. Great car. Let me tell you about several of the features of this new model. First of all, it has one of the highest crash safety test ratings due to the construction of the body and frame. It has been widely talked about in the industry."

Me: "I really don't need to know about crash test ratings. I'm sure most cars have safety features."

Car Salesperson: "So safety isn't important to you?"

Game over! He had eight seconds—you could have timed it—and he used them to alienate us. Talk about a crash test.

Yes, he really said those words. We literally had nothing else to say. We walked out. I hate to think how many people out there might have had to deal with this guy.

It all happens within those few seconds that follow greeting a potential customer. If you understand how to leverage those eight seconds properly by opening and engaging in a constructive peer-to-peer conversation, you can then begin the process of developing trust, which is perhaps the most vital piece of the effective retail selling process. Trust is what allows you to get to the real truth behind the customer's needs and wants.

You must know one thing for sure by now. Just saying, "Hi, can I help you?" (or any variation) is a sure bet for hearing, "No, thanks, I'm just looking," even if the prospect wants to buy something. If you are looking for a way to get the force fields up, to get the prospect to say nothing, to go into protective "I don't want to be sold" mode, you know exactly how to do that. Start the exchange by asking, "Can I help you?"

What does a successful interaction with a customer look like? Well, it might start with:

> "Hi, welcome to our store. Thanks for stopping in today."

Now here is the true pattern interrupt—something your prospect probably does not expect. Follow that with silence.

The silence will last only for a short period of time, perhaps two or three seconds. You will use that time wisely. There is a science when it comes to better understanding how your prospects engage (or not) at the onset of the interaction, and this silence gives you the opportunity to leverage that science.

You will now have the opportunity to observe your customer's response. Do they return a smile and a friendly "hello," or do they avoid eye contact and give off the implied zone of "leave me alone"? Either way, no problem. Just notice what you get back. Some people are strongly relationship-oriented. Some people are strongly task-oriented. What happens during your strategic decision to stop talking and notice the other person will give you an initial sense of which kind of person you're dealing with.

What's your goal now? Pretty simple: establish credibility while complementing what you have just figured out about whether this prospective buyer is relationship- or task-oriented.

Here's what the dictionary has to say about credibility:

Credibility: the quality of being trusted and believed in.

You can establish credibility in a very short period of time, provided that you respect the other person's communication style. Once you do establish credibility, once you demonstrate that you can communicate effectively and that you are committed to helping the buyer make the right decision even if that means you may not get this particular sale, the buyer is likely to surprise you with often disarming honesty.

Pretend I'm your customer. Why should I do business with you?

What makes you different? Better?

What would be the top three reasons I would consider doing business with you or your store?

Would it be:

- Your deep knowledge of your products and services?
- Your amazing, fabulous, extraordinary customer service?

- Your products or services themselves? After all, they are the finest, the best, most interesting, most creative, best things you have ever seen, right?

If you're like most of the retail sales professionals I work with, your answer to the question, "Why should I buy from you?" touched on one, two, or all three of these elements.

Now comes another question—a tougher one.

Are some, if not all, of these statements similar or identical to what your competitors are saying?

Are these responses creating true differentiation, separating you and your retail establishment from others who make similar claims in your marketplace? Are they giving your prospect or customer the impression that product knowledge, service, or product quality are really supposed to establish you as being different from and better than your competitors?

Bottom line: Those things do not establish credibility. So what does?

Let's define true credibility in the retail selling process.

Credibility is saying something seemingly not in your best interest prior to saying everything in your best interest. In other words, it is the path of creating disarming honesty between you and your prospect/customer.

Disarming Honesty = Credibility

Remember: People love to buy, yet hate to be sold.

Let me give an example of a personal shopping experience that illustrates this credibility concept powerfully.

I've always enjoyed the sport of skiing as a child and continue to love it as an adult. Some of my greatest memories with my wife and our two sons have come from spending time together on the slopes in the northeastern United States and also in the Rocky Mountains. We have done this over a period of many years. Recently, it had become apparent that I needed to look at buying some new equipment, such as skis and boots. I decided it was time to start looking and do the research.

I headed over to our local retail ski shop, where we had shopped for skis and boards for our sons for many years. I had been using the same equipment for several years and thought that perhaps this was the time to upgrade everything, including new boots. I started looking at a wide array of new skis, bindings, and new boots, some having up-to-date technology, updates to their design, and a higher than average price tag for all the additional cool stuff they offered.

After a few moments, I was greeted by one of the store's experienced sales guys. This salesperson, Kareem, used his eight seconds well. He welcomed me to the store, waited a few seconds, then asked what had brought me in that day. I said I was thinking about buying some new boots. He asked me about my current boots. He asked me about their make and age and why I thought it was time to look for new ones.

I answered at length. I was getting prepared for the official pitch, thinking he would now show me what I was looking for, the latest and greatest models of boots, after which he would start trying to sell me a whole lot of new ski equipment, including new boots. To my surprise, Kareem actually said, "Based on what you are describing about your boots, you may not have to replace them right now. If you would like to bring them in, I would be happy to take a look at them and see if an adjustment will be all that is needed right now. OK?"

Wait. What? You mean you're not trying to sell me new boots? Or new everything else? Why not?

Now that was a pattern interrupt. Not what I was expecting at all!

Credibility? Trust? Yes. Not only did my level of trust in him go up, I ended up spending a large amount of money on other items during that visit. As promised, Kareem did arrange to adjust my ski boots. All good. (I did end up going back after a few months to get new boots anyway. I'm glad I did.)

Where have I sent my friends after sharing this story with them? That's right. To that store—and Kareem. I have told this story to many friends since then. Some have visited the same store, looking for Kareem, knowing they, too, would be helped and not pressured.

This experience confirms what truly motivates buyers, especially when they walk in the door to a retail business. Are they there to just "look around" or is there a greater chance, if you provide them with just the right amount of rapport, engagement, and honest conversation while really creating credibility, that they could build a different kind of relationship with you? A relationship built on trust and a solid foundation of loyalty for years to come?

WHY MOST RETAIL BUYERS ARE ON THEIR GUARD

If you ask people about their very first impression of salespeople, you may not be surprised to learn that those impressions tend to be more negative than positive at first. Here are some samples of the words people instantly associate with salespeople:

- Pushy
- Aggressive
- Manipulative
- Fast talkers
- Not friendly—or too friendly
- Not that interested in the buyer and their needs

These initial thoughts bring on the zone of distrust and ultimately contribute to a challenging environment for the retail selling professional. They also lead the customer to refrain from telling the truth unless true credibility is established—and quickly.

In the world of retail selling as with selling in general, words such as *credibility*, *trust*, and *truth* are the essential elements in not only meeting but exceeding the expectations of the buyer. Often, credibility is missing. The customer's guard is up. This pattern leads to many instances where the prospect doesn't quite feel comfortable and, as a defense, maintains total control of the sales discussion. There is an irony here: When the prospect keeps complete control of the selling process, due to a lack of credibility and trust in their salesperson, they are likely to make poor decisions. For instance, they may evaluate up-front cost as being the single overriding factor and completely overlook issues like service or lifetime cost or product/service quality.

How to Establish Trust

Creating an open, unguarded, nurturing conversation with retail prospects by setting mutual expectations and helping them make their own discovery by means of thoughtful questions is the most effective way to sell.

Disarm the cycle of mistrust and replace it with an open environment of mutual comfort. This is what everyone wants as a customer: someone who is willing to see things from the customer perspective and guide them along the way.

"You are my friend when you walk in my shoes."
—*David Sandler*

THE THREE ELEMENTS OF COMMUNICATION: YOUR PATH TO CREDIBILITY

Your ability to establish credibility and secure trust is 100% dependent on the quality of your communication. The way to communicate with others can be broken into three separate elements:

- Body language.
- Tone.
- The spoken word.

Let's start by looking at body language and the many different messages it can convey. Make no mistake: physiology is communication. Are you using certain postures and physical displays that might make a buyer uneasy or defensive? Among these are:

- The semi-conscious choice to stand completely still.
- The inability to sustain relaxed, naturally dynamic eye contact.
- The decision to cover one's mouth with a hand, even briefly, while speaking.

Behavioral scientists, by the way, have identified all three of these as classic signals of dishonesty. I see retail sales personnel sending these signals constantly, and I bet you do, too. They put prospective buyers on edge and make it difficult or impossible for them to relax. Notice them! Avoid them! Other negative body signals include:

- Crossed arms.
- Hands hidden in pockets or behind back.
- Standing either too close or too far away from your prospect.
- Posture that appears to be closed or uninviting.
- Inappropriate physical contact.
- Facial expressions that appear unfriendly.

The other side of this coin is simple situational awareness. Start noticing and responding effectively to the body language and demeanor of customers who walk into your store or showroom.

- Do they make eye contact?
- Do they smile?
- Are their arms crossed, seemingly defensive in nature?
- Are they on their cell phones, ignoring you as they enter?
- Do they raise their hand or arm to indicate the non-verbal cue of "leave me alone"?

I find the study of physical space in our communication with others, the science of proxemics, fascinating. This is an extremely valuable aspect of rapport building.

Proxemics is the branch of knowledge that deals with the amount of space that people feel it necessary to set between themselves and others.

You may remember an episode of the classic television series *Seinfeld* about the "close talker" who gets on Jerry's nerves. Why did that episode resonate with so many people? Well, think of those times when people you had just been introduced to violated your physical space. How did that make you feel? In the retail selling world, you often meet people for the very first time. Here is a brief guide to help you gauge appropriate distance during conversations:

- Intimate distance: 0 to 2 feet
- Personal distance: 2 to 4 feet
- Social distance: 4 to 12 feet
- Public distance: more than 12 feet

I have seen many salespeople who were so eager to create effective bonding and rapport that they violated these general rules for the right distance. They were close talkers who lost the sale without even realizing why. To add insult to injury, some actually touched customers, either on the arm or using both hands, when greeting them for the very first time. Not a great plan. The way you use physical space should, first and foremost, keep people comfortable. Start out at about four feet away and then watch what happens. If the customer is receptive to your conversation and comfortable with you doing so, you can move in to about two feet—but certainly no closer. And keep your hands to yourself.

Next is tonality. When you speak to your prospective buyer, do you use a tone that matches theirs? (Remember: people buy from people they like and who are like them). Does your rate of speech match that of the other person?

(Ditto.) Do you vary your tone naturally? (A robotic mono-tone is a turnoff.) Is your voice relaxed? (Tension in your voice means tension in the relationship.)

Finally, let's focus on the spoken word itself, even though the words you use have less impact on the message you send than your physiology and your tonality. We've already examined the immense damage that can be done by phrases like, "Can I help you?" It's worth considering, too, how alienating any memorized recitation of features and benefits can be to the person on the receiving end. Those words kill sales.

BREAKING THE RETAIL BUYER'S BUBBLE

As we have seen, buyers are often guarded and on the defense when they walk in the door. They may tell us they are just looking and avoid eye contact. They could even pretend to be interested when they aren't, just to maintain a sense of control. This the what I call the retail buyer's "bubble." This protective force field is designed to shield the retail buyer from pressure, amateur selling moves, and the various unpredictable forms of manipulation mind games in which certain types of salespeople engage. The question is, how can you create mutual trust, comfort, and truthfulness in interactions with such buyers?

Typically, in an initial training session with a retail sales team, I demonstrate the concept of defensiveness and resistance by asking one participant to stand up, face me, and place their hands up against mine, which are raised to about chest height. I then begin to push, only to find them instantly pushing back. This is a subconscious and intuitive response. It happens almost every single time.

Next, I relax and ask the participant to place their hands in the same position they were in before. I calmly ask them to relax their hands. They do. Once I have suggested this new rule, I can then make contact and move my hands in any direction, while also helping them to move in sync with my movements. There is fearlessness and no resistance.

This is how I demonstrate to retail salespeople who attempt to forcefully sell through high pressure tactics that you must create a safe space. You must relax first and engage in a relaxed way. The pushing in the first example only brings defensiveness and pushing back. You can minimize resistance by creating an emotionally relaxed space for the emerging conversation, a place where the prospect can sense that you won't push too hard or create unnecessary pressure.

NEVER JUDGE A BOOK BY ITS COVER

Speaking of creating a safe space, let me tell you about one of my favorite retail customers ever.

He walked into my jewelry store with a purposeful stride, without meeting my gaze. He was an older gentleman, wearing a wrinkled shirt and jeans that were at least one size too large for him. His hair was unkempt. Frankly, he looked like a homeless person. As he walked in, he began looking in each of the showcases, pacing around the place with what looked like a mission and real purpose. I remembered my father's story about a similarly unprepossessing couple. After greeting him with "hello" and "welcome," I decided to give him a few moments of freedom to walk around the store.

In a few minutes, he asked for my advice about a gift choice. After some pleasant conversation and learning a little bit about him and what he was thinking, I helped him to decide on a pair of diamond earrings for his wife. It was a substantial purchase. At the cash register, when he took out his credit card, I was, I admit, momentarily curious about whether the sale would clear. It did. He received his gift-wrapped diamond earrings and gave me a warm smile. The smile seemed to say, "I'll be back." Indeed this was the first of many transactions from him. He recommended us to many friends and family members.

What if I had made a surface judgment? What if I had ordered him out of the store, based on his appearance alone? What if, instead of giving him the few moments of uninter-rupted searching he obviously needed, I had cornered him and pestered him with a list of qualifying questions?

In this case, rather than assume he couldn't afford any-thing in the store at all, I thought of the possibilities that might open up if I created a no-judgment zone. I decided to follow his lead.

Notice that following his lead was not the same as ignoring him. When he asked for help, I didn't make him feel that he was interrupting my busy day. I didn't send the message that keeping my shelves clean and restocked, checking inventory, or updating signage on the floor was more important than interacting with him. I made no assumptions; I gave him my undivided attention. That's what created a safe space. That's what made a nurturing interaction and actual communication possible.

———————

"No mind reading." —David Sandler

———————

A side note: In many cases, stores choose to have their salespeople do other important jobs and chores while they are working. Display, inventory, signage, administrative tasks, and responsibilities take precedence. Sales becomes an added chore to a long list of responsibilities. The stated culture of that retail establishment may claim the customer comes first, yet the sales team may not be hired and trained to truly see it that way—which means customers won't see it that way.

What this gentleman shared with me as I rang up his purchase was that this was the second store he had been to. The first store he walked into had beautiful merchandise, too; however, not even one salesperson greeted him as he walked in. Nothing. He even commented that people walked in after him, people who were dressed a little bit better than he was. He was astonished that again, no one even acknowledged him. He left without giving them his business and became one of my most loyal customers.

My father was right. You never really know what potential any customer might have. Every time you make an assumption about someone, you risk making the space feel less than safe. You risk losing a relationship.

Your customer is a guest in your home. Treat them that way. Instead of, "Can I help you?" consider saying:

"Hi. Welcome."

"Hi. Welcome to [store name]."

"Hi. Welcome to [store name]. I'm Rob. And you are...?" "Nice to meet you, Brian."

At this point, you can direct the conversation by observing your customer's unique response. Are they more focused on people or on the task at hand? Notice that predisposition, whatever it is. Follow the customer's lead.

Some people will simply want to cut to the chase and get right down to business, while others may want to engage in a bit more conversation up front to create a relationship within their own comfort zone.

At some point, you may find it appropriate to ask, "So, what brings you in today?"

Alternatively, you may find something that you can compliment. (This must be done sincerely.) I have found this to work because it encourages the customer to begin talking about themselves.

In my years as a retailer, I encouraged my team to compliment (genuinely!) a prospect's jewelry, necktie, shoes, or
other accessory. The rule here is that if the team member
doesn't agree that the item in question warrants a compliment, they don't mention anything. They have to really like
what they see.

"That's a beautiful pin you're wearing."

"Thank you. It was a gift from my students."

"Oh, you're a teacher. Where do you teach?"

And off you go. A new relationship begins!

It is important to set some boundaries around these kinds
of compliments. One of the off-limits areas is a person's
physical appearance or indeed anything that might be perceived as too personal. Invasive comments about hair, eyes,
and physical attributes can make people uncomfortable and
create the exact opposite reaction to the one you want. It's
also important to be careful about dealing with couples and
avoid the appearance of being too friendly with one over the
other. I have seen this create unintended discomfort, lost
opportunities, and hard feelings. Not what you are after!

Items it is appropriate to compliment authentically include:

- Shoes, accessories including handbags or brief-
  cases, watches, items of jewelry. (Don't comment

on how great a garment looks on someone; this can be misinterpreted.)

- Gadgets, cell phones, phone accessories, etc.
- Family. Other people, including children and older family members should be acknowledged.

I remember an excellent retail salesperson kneeling and speaking kindly to my son when he was just two years old. Imagine how a couple of proud parents felt about this. She was warm, engaging and professional. We could see she was capable of initiating a relationship in a very authentic and non-assuming way, and this created comfort for us. Our son didn't mind the attention, either. Talk about a great first impression.

SUMMARY

In this chapter, you learned a number of techniques to use within the critical first eight seconds of your interaction with a potential customer that can open the lines of communication. Don't just read about these techniques. Practice them and use them. Remember, you don't get a second chance to make a good first impression.

EIGHT

When 1+1=3, or Changing the Game

magine this scenario:

A customer walks into a retail establishment and is approached by a salesperson. Pleasantries are exchanged. Some brief questions lead to a presentation of some sort.

There's not much talking by the prospect, just a few pointed questions. The prospect then asks for a card, brochure, or other marketing material and proceeds to tell the salesperson they need to do their homework and research and will be back in touch. And they're gone.

This is something every salesperson has seen: "I'll be back." On the surface, everything is nice, pleasant, and respectful.

Yet the reality is these are not nice experiences for the retailer. They are lost opportunities.

Could it have turned out any differently?

Yes. There is a game-changing idea you can incorporate here: an idea that opens up the possibility of engaging in a deeper dialogue; an idea that allows you to create nurturing in the exchange before the prospect walks out the door; an idea that makes it possible to create comfort, trust, and engagement—while this person is still in the store.

When people tell you they need to "think it over," when they tell you "I'll be back," you usually don't know the reasons behind the prospect's decision to shut down the conversation. It's a communication breakdown. Could a lack of connection or a failure of person-to-person chemistry cause this shutdown? Inquiring minds want to know! There's one great way to find out—and it's a game-changer.

In their quest to create an effective retail shopping experience, many successful managers and retail owners have focused on a team selling model. This model can create an environment of more openness and engagement from buyers who would otherwise slip into "I'll be back" mode.

Let's face it. From time to time, there just isn't any chemistry between a given buyer and a given salesperson. Why not notice when this is happening, take a team approach, and let someone else—a manager or a colleague—walk over and take over the sale? This step opens the possibility of resurrecting an engaged, nurturing conversation with the prospect. It harnesses the potential synergy of the team on the sales floor. In this case, one salesperson plus one salesperson can equal a whole lot more than two salespeople. It can equal unlimited possibility.

I have met with many companies where it is mandated that within 10 to 15 minutes of a sales interaction that does not seem to be productive, if the salesperson does not release the opportunity to another salesperson, they may be disciplined, or, in more extreme cases, terminated. That sounds harsh, I know, but consider the goal: to create a nurturing relationship leading to the customer feeling enough trust and comfort to buy. If there aren't clear signs of that happening with one salesperson, the responsibility for leading the discussion goes to someone else.

I see this kind of team selling as a pure benefit to both the company and the customer, given the right scenario and a supportive working culture. A typical high-pressure environment will not support this team selling approach. For it to work, the environment must be customer-focused, rather than self-focused.

The guiding principle here is a simple one: New face, new opportunity. There are a number of ways to execute a successful take over. For instance:

- **Ask the expert.** "Dina has a lot of expertise in this area. Let me bring her over and ask her to help us."
- **Second opinion.** "Why don't I invite Mary over here to get her opinion?" This can be extremely effective

with an indifferent or undecided prospect who might otherwise leave the store out of simple confusion.

- **Take two.** In this variation, the manager (or someone else) simply joins the conversation, seemingly unbidden, in a tactful and subtle way, and asks appropriate questions to "restart" the conversation from scratch.

I remember one of my sales team members, Kay, had a real talent for staying nearby when a customer speaking with another salesperson appeared uncertain about a purchase. Kay was a very attentive listener while not disrupting or intervening at all during the conversation. She'd notice when the conversation was beginning to become distant, and she would demonstrate true team selling at this moment. Her timing was usually perfect. She would simply walk over and say, "You know, I haven't seen how this looks on you. Would you mind trying it on again, please?"

The result? A fresh approach, a new face, and another opportunity to help the customer would always increase the chances that this customer would be comfortable with their purchase.

I can remember one particular case where a nervous and unsure prospect become a reassured and happy customer, thanks to Kay's quiet, seamless intervention in the conversation. Everybody won. My store kept a sale (it was a beautiful necklace), the team enjoyed a shared bonus, and, most importantly, our customer left the store feeling great about their purchase.

I call the guiding principle behind the take-over strategy 1+1=3. This simple mnemonic reinforces the core idea that, in a team selling environment, the whole really can be greater than the sum of its parts. It's true that you never get a second chance to make a good first impression. However, it's also true that team selling gives you the opportunity to overcome a less-than-ideal first impression, replace it with something better, and reduce the number of "be backs" that come about simply because a given prospect and a given salesperson didn't connect.

SUMMARY

The 1+1=3 strategy will help you turn around situations where a customer might otherwise have left the store without making a purchase. It's a game changer. Use it!

NINE

Comfort and Mutual Understanding: The Up-Front Agreement

As discussed previously, successful relationships, ultimately leading to sales, happen because people tend to buy from people they like and who are like them. A critical goal in supporting such a relationship is creating a nurturing atmosphere of trust, mutual comfort, and understanding. To accomplish this, the best way is to set mutual expectations.

In other words, resist the urge to immediately begin

selling to the customer. Setting realistic expectations creates comfort first, so that must happen early in the discussion.

I remember a situation involving a local bank several years ago. I was a customer. As their policy of being customer-focused required, they made it a point to have their team members greet their customers as they entered the bank. The thinking was that everyone would feel special as they were greeted as they entered the door. Harmless enough, I guess.

On this particular day, I remember their greeting and a very long line. I also remember a feeling of not having a lot of time to get my banking done. One of the bank representatives asked if I wanted to step into one of the offices to take care of my banking.

Would I mind? Of course not.

She ushered me into one of the cubicles where a very polite assistant manager welcomed me and asked for me to sit down while she would take care of my deposit.

Out of the blue, she asked me, "Where do you invest your money?"

I wasn't sure if that was exactly what I heard so I asked her to repeat it. "Excuse me?" I asked.

She then repeated her question. "Where do you invest your money?"

My first thought was, *Why would I tell you?* or maybe it was, *That's none of your business!* (Wouldn't one of those responses be your reaction?) Not a great initial impression.

Maybe they imagined that the greeting at the door gave them the right to ask personal questions without any warning.

But suppose she had taken a different approach? Suppose she had said, "Mr. Fishman, thank you for being a customer of ABC Bank. Many of our customers ask us about ways to enhance their investment portfolios. I am sure yours has done well so far and that you are most likely in good hands. Would you mind if I asked you a few brief questions about your finances and investment strategies in order to see whether or not we should speak further? It will only take a few moments."

If she had said something like that, I believe I might have had a very different initial reaction. I might have gotten into the discussion, starting a disarming and truthful dialogue—and perhaps a selling opportunity for her and a better investment opportunity for me. Unfortunately, that didn't happen.

In many other settings, I see many salespeople make the same mistake. They jump into interrogation mode right from the start.

Typically, the issue of budget is brought up ridiculously early. This is not to say that it isn't important to talk about money at some point—it is. But remember that your aim is to make people feel comfortable. There isn't much comfort created by posing awkward questions within seconds of striking up a conversation, such as: "How much do you want to spend?" or "What's your budget?"

Too many salespeople jump into awkward mode by asking

probing questions without taking any time to measure the comfort level of their prospect. I have seen this on countless occasions. Personable salespeople, who really do want to help, can make customers and prospects very uncomfortable without even realizing it. If you want to immediately disarm and create mutual comfort in the sales process, you must get into the habit of asking permission before you start asking such questions. This request for permission helps to remove the prospect's defensive stance and replace it with comfort and openness to having a real conversation.

Here's what it might sound like. "Do you mind if I ask you a few questions to get a sense of how I might be able to help you?" This technique, originated by David Sandler, is technically known as an Up-Front Contract. In the retail environment, I call it an Up-Front Agreement. Whatever you call it, it sets the ground rules.

Would most people mind if you were to ask some questions? No. Most would not mind. Most people will say something like, "Sure, go ahead." Everyone stays calm and relaxed.

The up-front agreement is designed to create mutual comfort and remove perceived pressure arising from any interaction with you. The goal is to begin the process of having a more relaxed, informative and ultimately more gratifying shopping experience for your customer. Period. If you aren't already using this kind of agreement, start. Here are the key steps of introducing such an agreement, designed specifically for the retail selling professional.

- **Appreciation.** Show appreciation and welcome them. There are lots of ways to do this. For instance, "Thanks for stopping in today. We appreciate the opportunity to help you with what you might be looking for."
- **Silence.** Wait for a couple of seconds to see what happens.
- **Name.** If the customer seems receptive, say: "My name is Rob. And you are...?"
- **Agreement.** "I'd be happy to help you with what you are looking for. Would it be OK with you if I ask you some questions to get a better understanding?" (Wait for a response.)
- **Reciprocity.** "Obviously, you might also have questions for me. I'd be happy to answer them for you."
- **Transition into a question.** For instance, "Tell me more about what you're looking for today."

Note: No hard sell!

If your goal is to create mutual comfort, and it is, also let your prospect know that, although you are very good at what you do, you know you might not be right for everyone. There is no pressure. Let the customer know up front that if it turns out to be a *no*, it is OK to let you know that. Tell them that right out loud. That may seem counterintuitive. It is meant to be. This is not something the prospect is expecting. It covers a problem rarely addressed in most sales interactions: the feeling that the salesperson somehow disapproves of the prospect if the answer is *no*. This is not a grown-up perspective. Say clearly and explicitly that there will be no hard sell.

Note that this is a flexible model. There is more than one right way to do it. Here is another variation of an initial greeting, leading to an up-front agreement.

Welcome and Name. **Salesperson:** "Hi, welcome. My name is Rob."

Customer: "Hi, Rob, I'm Naira and this is Phil. We'd like to get some information on men's dress watches." (Note that there is no need to wait for a second here, because the customer has initiated the dialogue.)

Agreement. **Salesperson:** "I would be happy to help you. Do you mind if I ask the both of you some questions in order to get a better idea of what specifically you might be looking for?"

Customer: "Sure."

Reciprocity and transition into a question. **Salesperson:** "I'll do my best to answer any questions you might have. Can you tell me a little more about..." You could ask how they heard about your store, or why they are asking what they are asking regarding that specific item. The possibilities are limitless. (You'll learn more about effective questioning in Chapter 11.)

Notice that this is a permission-based model of retail selling. Not only does it create comfort and trust, it also sets the stage for an honest, open, and friendly exchange of information, facilitating the discovery process for both you and your customer. Permission is a critically important phase of the sales interaction, and it should happen shortly after the initial greeting.

SUMMARY

Don't rush into the information-gathering phase of the sale. Get permission by creating a clear agreement up front about the ground rules and what will take place during the discussion. This technique is worth practicing until you attain the level of mastery; it will change the entire dynamic of conversations with your prospects.

TEN

Finding the
Right Customer

Who is the right customer? I say it is the one who is *qualified* to be your customer: the person who has a problem you can solve and who is willing and able to purchase from you. In other words, there is a clear reason for them to buy, and they have the money and decision-making power to do so.

Let's reverse engineer this to another question. Are you the right salesperson? Take a moment and think of the kind of salesperson you aspire to be. There are basically two possibilities in retail.

The cookie-cutter or one-size-fits-all salesperson is selling the same way to all possible styles of people, all the time. The professional salesperson, on the other hand, learns about the way in which one individual prospect acts, speaks, thinks, and ultimately, communicates. I hope you agree with me by now that, in order to approach the right customer, it helps to be that second kind of salesperson.

With that much understood, let's take a look at what you need to uncover in order to be certain that a prospect is truly qualified to be the right customer:

- **Their reason to buy.** Is there a specific need or problem? Is there a situation that would create a gap between where the prospect is currently and their desired outcome? This could be something as simple as a want or desire for a brand-new pair of shoes, or a handbag, or a large TV, or the latest gadget. Here are some examples of this gap and some possible reasons behind them:

  - Your customer is looking for and also motivated to buy a new car. What you may not know yet is the reason they are shopping: Their current model is older and has needed many repairs recently, and that is frustrating to them.
  - Your customer is considering working on home improvement and has been talking to decorators and remodelers. What you may not know yet is that, deep down, they are self-conscious and concerned over the current appearance of their home

and its décor. They feel it's dated, and they aren't happy with the way it looks in comparison with other homes.

* Your customer is a soon-to-be married couple, looking at engagement rings. Of course, the obvious reason they are in your store is that they are in love and looking to commit to each other. What you may not know yet is that they are each concerned about whether they are making the right decision about the wedding bands they choose. With so many choices and prices, it is common for such customers to be overwhelmed. They're looking for guidance in locating the right balance between appearance and value.

* Your customer is looking for a gift for a spouse. What you may not know is that they had a disappointing experience at your main competitor's store.

You don't know any of those underlying reasons, and you need to know that you don't know. Remember, no mind reading. You can't make assumptions based on your experiences with past customers. Each customer is different.

- **Budget.** There are basically two things you need to find some way to confirm once the customer is comfortable enough to discuss them with you:

- Able: Do they have the ability to pay?
- Willing: Do they see real value in what you are offering?

- **Decision making.** In the world of retail selling, the decision might be up to a one-person "committee." In other cases, you might be talking to a couple, one of whom is eager to purchase and the other is more resistant. Failing to establish a meaningful dialogue with each person can lead to "be back" responses, like, "Let us think about it," "What are your hours?" and "May we have your card please?"

Having a clear sense of where the customer stands in all three areas helps both of you make the best possible decisions. It also allows you to be efficient with your precious time and energy, focusing your attention on those customers who meet clear criteria for qualification. Spending time and energy on unqualified buyers is a strategic mistake.

Your Hidden Decision Maker: The Internet

With the increasing use of social media and websites that provide analysis of pricing and the buying experience, many buyers now turn to the web to gather input and feedback on you and your brand. Think of your own personal experience with a recent major purchase. Did you look up customer reviews of either the product, the store selling it, or competitors? How much influence do these social media posts and websites have on your buying process?

Your prospect or customer may well consult the same sources. The savvy retail sales professional is aware of the influence these resources can play. (By the way, the increasing popularity of these sites is one reason you don't want to deliver a negative customer experience and then leave it unresolved. These days, the details of such disputes tend to end up online, damaging your store's reputation.)

If you don't know what people are saying about your store online, find out.

UNDERSTANDING THEIR (AND YOUR) TRUE COMMUNICATION STYLE

I'll say it again: People buy from people they like and who are like them. Specifically, they buy from people they like who can communicate like they do in a way that makes them comfortable.

My own goal is to blend in with the prospect. If, for example, they speak slowly and softly, I would do the same. If they do not make any eye contact, I would respectfully restrain from staring them down, which might make them uncomfortable. The goal here is to make the environment comfortable for your prospect by paying careful attention to them and their style and adjusting accordingly. This will take some practice. You might even make some mistakes at first. Keep trying until you master this and make it a habit.

One great way to accelerate the learning curve is to become familiar with the DISC model, a behavior assessment tool based on the DISC theory of psychologist William Moulton Marston. DISC centers on four different personality traits: Dominant (D), Influencer (I), Steady Relator (S), and Compliant (C).

You'll recall that, a little earlier in this book, I advised you to start noticing whether people walking into your store were more focused on relationships or on completing tasks. This is a natural preference that will start to jump out at you the more you start observing people and looking for it. DISC is based on two such natural preferences. The first, task orientation as opposed to people orientation, can be pretty obvious once you learn to spot it. The second is (for me) even easier to notice: Is the person more of an introvert or an extrovert? Understanding these two tendencies is the key to understanding and using the DISC tool.

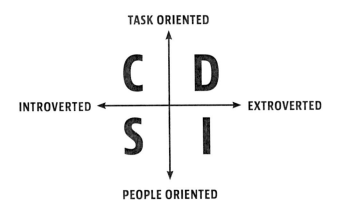

To get the most out of DISC, a truly transformative resource, it helps to start by identifying your own personal style.

Take this short, simple quiz to begin getting a sense of what style you are most like. At first, pay attention only to the left-hand column you see below.

Step I

For each group of words, use the numbers 1, 2, 3, and 4. Assign ratings to yourself for each of the words in each group. The number 4 will be the descriptor that is most like you; 3 will be a descriptor that is nearly like you; 2 will be a descriptor that is somewhat or less like you; and 1 will be the descriptor that is least like you. Each group of words must have all of the rankings: 4, 3, 2, and 1. By the way, there are no right or wrong answers. Please answer the way you believe you behave and not the way you think you should answer.

A.		Bold	D
		Enthusiastic	I
		Friendly	S
		Conscientious	C
B.		Outspoken	D
		Attractive	I
		Good-natured	S
		Logical	C

C.		Daring	D
		Outgoing	I
		Agreeable	S
		Careful	C
D.		Strong-willed	D
		Charming	I
		Sympathetic	S
		Tactful	C
E.		Pioneering	D
		Talkative	I
		Gentle	S
		Well-disciplined	C
F.		Competitive	D
		Good mixer	I
		Even-tempered	S
		Thorough	C
G.		Dominant	D
		Sociable	I
		Easygoing	S
		Controlled	C
H.		Direct	D
		Appealing	I
		Kind	S
		Reserved	C
I.		Vigorous	D
		High-spirited	I
		Amiable	S
		Accurate	C

J.		Restless	D
		Expressive	I
		Considerate	S
		Diplomatic	C

Step 2

Now, looking at the column that contains the letters DISC, add up the values that you placed in each group. For example, in group A, you may have entered these numbers in the following order, ranging from what is most like you (4) down to what is least like you (1)

A.	2	Bold	2	D
	1	Enthusiastic	1	I
	4	Friendly	4	S
	3	Conscientious	3	C

Step 3

Add up all the D, I, S, and C numbers. Enter the totals below:

_____D _____I _____S _____C

When you have completed all three steps, your four scores should total 100. Circle the letter with the highest point total. Now circle the letter with the second highest score. The letter that connects to your highest score is, in all likelihood, your primary DISC communication style. The second highest score is likely to correspond with your secondary DISC profile score. (Most people score highly in two DISC areas, with one area significantly more pronounced than the other.)

Let me repeat: There are no good or bad scores here. This quick quiz is designed to give you a general sense of what your preferred communication style might be. The experienced and well-versed sales professional knows how to adapt their natural style to fit that of the prospect or customer, creating a mutually comfortable and effective selling process.

One of the best ways to begin qualifying your customer is to better understand how they communicate and to communicate with them in a way that seems natural to them. This lowers their defensive guard, lets them open up, and allows you to help them. Why is understanding these communication styles so important in the sales process? Because the ability to create and sustain rapport with prospects and begin conversations effectively depends on complementing these styles, rather than fighting with them. Understanding your own style and being willing to adapt it to suit your prospect's is an essential first step.

Let's take a closer look at the four distinctively different, yet related, styles of people.

Dominant: These people are direct, decisive, competitive, and goal-oriented self-starters. They get right to the point. They are bottom-line oriented and big-picture focused. Most are task driven and blunt—sometimes to a fault.

Here is what you may hear and observe from a high Dominant buyer:

"Give me your best price."

"What's the bottom line?"

"I'm in a rush."

"How much is it?"

"Your competitor is less expensive. Why should I buy from you?"

How to communicate with high Dominant buyers:

- Be direct, brief, and to the point.
- Focus on the task; stick to business.
- Use a results-oriented approach.
- Identify opportunities/challenges.
- Ensure they win.
- Offer solutions and alternatives.
- Touch on high points; don't overuse data.
- Be aware of personal space.
- Do not be emotional; do not dominate.
- Act quickly; they are quick decision makers.

The high Dominant's biggest fear is loss of control. Let them drive the conversation.

Don't assume they want to socialize. They don't. Lose the chitchat. Dominants may lack diplomacy and tact at times.

In other words, they may not come off as friendly at first. Don't let that throw you.

Famous high Dominants: General George S. Patton, Jack Nicholson, Jerry Seinfeld.

Influencer: These people are relationship-driven and great with people. They are charming, confident, inspiring, persuasive, sociable, friendly, optimistic, engaging, talkative, and expressive. They love small talk.

Here is what you may hear and observe from a high Influencer buyer:

"My friend/relative speaks highly of you and your store."

"Nice to meet you. Where are you from?"

"What do you think of this color?"

"Do you know [naming people]?"

When interacting with these buyers, you will notice lots of eye contact, plenty of warmth, boatloads of engaging conversation, and many questions. They are talkative folks. They are easy to have a conversation with.

How to communicate with high Influencer buyers:

- Converse freely and make sure there is plenty of time to socialize.
- Lighten up and have some fun.
- Ask for feelings and opinions.
- Smile and be animated.

- Be friendly and warm, paying plenty of personal attention.
- Express genuine enthusiasm.
- Let them speak.
- Give them recognition.
- Talk about people and feelings.
- Accept that conversations may include many seemingly unrelated topics: family, where you live, children, pets, current events, people you may know in common, and even your favorite dining places.

The high Influencer's biggest fear is not being liked. Many have a high need for approval, even from new acquaintances.

Influencers can sometimes be inattentive to details and unrealistic in appraising people. They value interaction and relationships highly; they are likely to need to hear the opinions of others before making a decision. Take that into account when making a recommendation.

Famous high Influencers: Will Smith, Robin Williams, Oprah Winfrey.

Steady Relator: These folks are team players who generally avoid conflict. They are supportive, friendly, patient, amiable, sincere, optimistic, sympathetic, and understanding. They are likely to avoid putting all their cards on the table, not because they are out to mislead anyone, but because they don't like causing trouble. They are pleasant. Like high Influencers, high Steady Relators tend to be relationship-driven.

Here is what you may hear and observe from a high Steady Relator:

"I need some help with..."

"What would you recommend or suggest to me in regards to...?"

"My friend had shopped here and mentioned your name."

"I appreciate your help."

As a broad but generally accurate rule, Steady Relators are kind, courteous, and mostly calm. To communicate effectively with them in a retail setting, you should:

- Be patient, and build trust over time.
- Draw out their opinion in an extended conversation. Don't demand an opinion early in the relationship. (This is very important!)
- Become an ally, no matter what the purchase decision is.
- Respect the person's need to consult with friends and family members.
- Present the situation in a logical way, without a lot of drama.
- Relax and allow plenty of time for discussion.
- Slow down. Provide all the information they need.
- Secure mini-commitments along the way.

The high Steady Relator's biggest fear is fear of change. Truth be told, they can be resistant to anything that appears to upset the status quo. I have found the Steady Relator style to be the most challenging to identify, at least at first. It may be by default that you discover this style, after the realization that your prospect isn't any of the other styles. (One tipoff may be the emergence of polite nods and words of appreciation, after a slow start to the conversation.)

It may be quite difficult to establish what is happening with Steady Relators and how they really feel about you and the items you are selling. After all, they are very nice people. They may choose to not share everything about how they feel with what you are selling; they may not want to tell you if you are on the right track when it comes to helping them—that might cause a disagreement! Note that, more than the other three styles, this group is averse to direct conflict. They play their cards close to the vest, and do not like being pressured.

Famous high Steady Relators: Mahatma Gandhi, Mother Teresa, Mr. Rogers.

Compliant: As the name suggests, these people are highly compliant with established systems, processes, and procedures. They are likely to expect the same approach from others. They are cautious, analytical, accurate, precise, conscientious, and patient. They focus on data and logic. Think Mr. Spock from *Star Trek*. Like high Dominants, high Compliants are task driven.

Because they can never get enough data, what you hear

and observe from the high Compliant will typically be a variation on this:

"I would like to see more specifics/details/data."

High Compliants may be the easiest of the four groups to spot quickly because they are almost always interested in gathering data. What does the warrantee say? What are the specifications? How has quality and durability been tested or certified? This is the group that is likeliest to have done online research before walking into your store. They are highly informed.

I once had a conversation with a prospective customer who was looking at an expensive Swiss watch. He was extremely interested in things like watch movement, accuracy specifications, water resistance certification, dimensions, and so on. What he really did not care about were the elements of fashion, style, and appearance. He was into the inner workings. He wanted all the details about the design and engineering and stress testing; he didn't care about the fluff or the marketing superlatives. He wanted to make sure he knew exactly what each sub-dial did (there were three) and the best way to wind this watch. He was a classic high Compliant—so I gave him all the information (and looked up that which I didn't have on hand). He ended up buying an extremely expensive watch. It was the first of several upscale watch purchases he made with us over the years. All of the subsequent models had to have all the same background information before he made his purchase. I had lots of research to do with each model! I did it because that's what was important to him. He became a loyal customer.

To communicate effectively with high Compliants in a retail setting, you should:

- Use data and facts.
- Keep on task.
- Proceed logically.
- Focus on long-term quality.
- Respect personal space.
- Be patient.
- Slow down.
- Keep small talk and personal sharing to a minimum.
- Explain the details carefully.
- Be prepared to do some research to support the relationship.

The high Compliant's biggest fear is being incorrect. They will invest the time necessary to learn what they need to learn to make the best decision. Become their ally in this effort. Avoid offering opinions. Stick to verifiable, documented facts. Stay on the logical side of the discussion.

Famous high Compliants: Bill Gates, Diane Sawyer, Albert Einstein.

It's likely that you have now spotted your own style. Great! Understand, though, that this is only the beginning. In a retail setting, it is important to be able to identify and adapt to the styles of other people quickly and efficiently. My guess is that you already feel quite comfortable communicating with people who share your style and that you can remember plenty of times when you have clicked with such customers. But do you really want to lose the other 75% of the market to your competition?

Using DISC to Make the First Impression Great

Here's where the rubber meets the road. Can you use the DISC model to improve your first eight seconds (and the critical few minutes that follow) with a prospective buyer? The short answer is an emphatic "yes."

Here are some examples of each group's likely mindset as they walk in the door of your store. Study these mindsets now, and start looking for them. They will help you discover the prospect's communication style. (Again: If you don't notice any significant style, you are most likely dealing with a Steady Relator.)

Dominant mindset: "I have a lot to do. Just give me the information I need. Don't waste my time. Cut to the chase."

Influencer mindset: "I've heard great things about you/this product/this store. I can't wait to show this to my friends."

Steady Relator mindset: "I like to ask my close friends/ family members for suggestions on where to shop for [product]." (Note that this person may not say much of anything at first.)

Compliant mindset: "I've looked online at the specifications of each model," followed by a technical question.

Now, here are your likely next steps with each group:

Dominant: These are the people who are most likely to walk in, get to the bottom line, and buy. Don't get in the way of that. People who offer lots of facts and figures to Dominant buyers are basically running a sales prevention department by talking too much and sabotaging what could be a very positive start to the sale. They tend to move quickly. So should you.

Influencer: Engage, engage, engage! Let them discover. Talk with them. Talk about family. Talk about friends. Become one of those friends. Make the connection.

Steady Relator: Think long term. Accept that these folks might not buy on the first trip. It is therefore vital that you make a great first impression and build comfort in the relationship. Respect their need to process information slowly and conduct all due diligence. The goal is to make a friend, build trust, and become part of their network. Do not write these people off. Steady Relator buyers have consistently become great referral sources for me and have led to significant new opportunities.

Compliant: These buyers are likely to step back and tell you they need some time to ponder, think, process and do their homework. Do not pressure them. Allow them that time, offering the statistical and other resources they need to discover the facts for themselves. Depending on the size of the transaction, you may decide that it makes sense to volunteer to help with the research and fact-finding.

We've already addressed the principle that people buy from people they like and from people who are like them. Adapting effectively to another person's DISC communication style is how you put this principle into practice. It's also the single best way to distinguish yourself from online competitors who never interact with the buyer in person.

Here are a few scenarios to consider.

Assume the customer is a Dominant and the salesperson is an Influencer. What if the salesperson doesn't change their communication style? They remain talkative, enthusiastic, smiling, socially focused. Now let's look at our prospective buyer. As a Dominant, this person is direct, to the point, bottom-line oriented, task-focused. How do you think the prospective customer would describe this salesperson? Maybe something like this: "Talked too much. In my face. Annoying." Not the ideal recipe for creating rapport!

Here's another example. Assume the customer is a Steady Relator. Assume the salesperson is a Dominant. The Steady Relator buyer is patient, calm, friendly, people-focused.

The Dominant salesperson, however, is direct, to the point, straightforward, task-focused. Again: Assuming the salesperson makes no effort to adapt to the other person's communication style, how do you think the customer is going to describe this salesperson? Probably something like this: "Pushy, aggressive, arrogant, in my face."

Case closed. If you were looking for a way to sabotage those critical first eight seconds of the relationship, you just found it: ignore the other person's preferred communication pattern and assume it's their job to learn to speak your language. On the other hand, if you want to make the most of those first few seconds and the minutes that follow, you can start noticing, start adapting, and start communicating in a way that makes people think, "Hey, I like coming here. People get me."

UNDERSTAND PRIMARY AND SECONDARY DISC STYLES

Now let's raise the bar to look at primary as well as secondary styles. Some people (a minority) operate using a combination of these styles with a somewhat higher reliance on a given style being listed first, as the primary style. Here are the possible combinations, and a brief description of each:

- DI or ID: Direct, yet talkative and engaging.
- IS or SI: Extremely people oriented; open, talkative, and attentive.
- SC or CS: Mostly indirect communication; highly process driven.

- CD or DC: Task driven; big-picture driven, while seeing the details at the same time.

Here again, the goal is to get good at spotting the style and adapting to it—or at least not challenging it. I must repeat the point yet again: There is no right or wrong DISC style. There is just how people operate. You either understand them and accommodate their communication preferences, or you don't. If you don't, you are basically telling them, "Please go shop elsewhere, and tell your friends and family to do the same."

It should always be considered your job to adapt your style to theirs. It does take practice. But that investment of time, energy, and attention is definitely worth it because it makes deep, rapid rapport possible with the customer.

Selling to couples is perhaps the ultimate test of your DISC skills. Now, instead of just one customer, there are two people who most likely know each other quite well and have made purchases together before walking into your store. Although it's certainly possible to find two people who are similar in style, it's more common to encounter differences in the way they communicate. One person may be eager to "just get down to business," while the other may want some chitchat first. Your goal as a sales professional is to create an inviting environment for both, which can be tricky at times.

Here's a possible scenario. A married couple walks into your store. She is a Dominant. He is a Steady Relator. She appears to be very direct and to the point, asking questions and steering the conversation, while her spouse seems more subdued, deferring to his partner and letting her do most of the talking about the potential purchase. You are answering her questions, and (you think) giving great information to both of them. All is apparently going great. Then you hear this: "Thank you for your time. You have been very helpful to us. Let us give this some thought, and we will be back."

You respond with, "Sure. No problem at all. When should I check back with you?"

They reply with, "Next week is good. Monday morning. Here's our phone number. May we have your card, please?"

You give them your card, knowing that you have a next step of calling them on Monday. Sounds promising, right?

That's when they enter the retail customer witness-protection program.

You leave voicemail after voicemail. No response. This goes on for weeks. Finally, with some good old perseverance, you find out they have changed their mind. Sound familiar? Most retail salespeople I've worked with tell me this kind of thing has happened to them many times.

Here are some dynamics that might have affected this exchange:

- The Steady Relator did not get the opportunity to be heard or express his own opinion during the interaction, leaving him feeling unserved as a customer and ultimately creating doubt.

- The Dominant may have had her own unexpressed

doubts, even though she was very expressive. You never found out what they were.

- You may have missed the mark by not setting a quick up-front agreement or by not asking questions that uncovered the couple's true concerns, preferences, and reasons for coming into the store in the first place.

All too often, the retail salesperson chooses to speak with the more outspoken or vocal of the two people, leaving the calmer, more subdued person without the opportunity to share their own opinions during the discussion. In the case of a Steady Relator, this person typically will not share opinions until they have been acknowledged, included in the conversation, made to feel safe, and asked to contribute. You must address both people, keeping in mind their different communication styles and the best ways to adapt to each. Here is an example:

"Tamara, I appreciate your letting me know about [whatever]. Jim, I was hoping you might share what you like about what Tamara has pointed out and if there is anything additional you might add about what you prefer. Any thoughts?"

It is vital that you make an effort to keep Jim comfortable, include him in the conversation and draw out his opinion. This may take more than one attempt, because, as a Steady Relator, Jim is so nice. He may say one thing, but feel something very different—and not share it with you because he doesn't like making a scene. It might take a little effort for you to get him to open up about his concerns and preferences. One thing is certain, though: Ignoring him altogether is not a great strategy. If you don't include him in the conversation in your store, you certainly won't be able to influence the (inevitable) conversation that happens when they leave.

ENGAGE!

Engagement really is the name of the game in retail. Now that you've heard about some of the most effective ways to create comfort as you approach people, let's summarize the best ways to engage with your prospect or customer as the relationship begins. Here is a helpful overview.

E-N-G-A-G-E

- **E:** Embrace each opportunity with consistency and purpose. Your job is to help another person get what they want. Period.
- **N:** No preconceptions. Never prejudge anyone, ever. Don't make assumptions about people and what motivates them. Be curious.
- **G:** Greet people professionally with a smile and friendly demeanor. Smile authentically.
- **A:** Ask permission to pose certain questions to get a better sense of what they are looking for.
- **G:** Gauge their DISC communication style early on.

Then adapt your own communication accordingly. Yes, this takes practice. It's worth it!

- E: Exceed their expectations. Call it the "wow!" factor. Call it whatever you want. Go above and beyond the call. This leads to more raving fans, more introductions, and a steady flow of prospects who become customers more easily.

SUMMARY

Spend your precious time and energy on qualified buyers.

Understand and master the DISC communication model. It will help you to connect with customers in a way that makes them feel comfortable. This is the single best way to distinguish from online competitors, who never interact with the buyer in person.

Master the ENGAGE model to improve your interactions with customers.

ELEVEN

Questioning Strategies

ffective questioning is all about following the "No mind reading" selling principle I shared with you a little earlier. This concept connects powerfully to the task of improving your listening skills, which in turn connect powerfully to your ability to create good conversations with a given customer.

While I was growing up, my parents often said to me: "You were given two ears and one mouth. You should be listening twice as much as speaking." Too many retail salespeople ignore this advice. They are far more interested in telling than they are in selling. Selling is actually all about listening and asking good questions based on what you hear. Telling is what usually happens. Why does this problem exist? Why is it so widespread?

Why is it that so many people in sales do too much talking, pitching, and telling, and hardly any listening at all?

One of the answers lies in the culture of learning provided by many organizations. Often, retail salespeople are trained in things like:

- Products
- Pricing
- Procedures
- Guarantees or warranties
- Services
- Competition and the key differences

On the other hand, they are given no training at all in how to conduct an effective conversation with a customer. So instead of selling, they tell.

The telling world consists of a mostly one-way conversation in which the retail salesperson explains how wonderful, exotic, or amazing their product or service is. This information typically comes by way of extensive amounts of product training and inevitably leads to lots of demonstrations, explanations, and eloquently delivered monologues by an experienced (but not very effective) salesperson. These monologues overwhelm many prospects—quite the opposite of what the salesperson was hoping to accomplish. The results: mediocre at best.

The selling world, by contrast, focuses on one area that differentiates mediocre selling from what I call legendary selling: the ability to ask effective questions to get a retail customer to do most of the talking. Using a guideline of a 70/30 ratio, where the customer or prospect speaks 70% of the time and the retail salesperson a corresponding 30%, amazing things begin to happen. The salesperson actually helps the customer make an effective decision by simply listening closely to what they are saying (or, in many cases, not saying).

This cannot happen without effective listening skills. Listening well is the only way to get the customer to do more talking and the only way to create a deeper level of understanding. Good listening actually begins with learning effective initial questioning strategies and skills and then listening and responding effectively to what comes back.

For example, here are some great opening questions:

"What's the special occasion?"

"So, what brings you into our store today?"

"What have you seen before that you [or he, or she] liked?"

"What's important to you [or them] in selecting this particular item?"

"Have you been handed any clues about something that would be special for her [or him]?"

And, one of my favorites, a mini up-front agreement:

"Would you mind if I ask you a few brief questions to make sure I understand exactly what you are looking for?"

With questions like these, your prospect will most likely take comfort in your interest and respond positively. The way they respond may tell you something about the reasons for the visit—and also about the DISC style of the buyer you're interacting with. You can now ask additional questions based on what you've heard from this unique customer and continue the process of learning more about them and helping them. Notice that there is no cookie-cutter or list of questions that works for every situation.

Let's look at why this approach is so effective. First of all, it establishes mutual respect and begins the process of building rapport and trust. Remember, people buy from people they like and who are like them. Establishing respect and rapport in the relationship is a critical part of that. In addition, this approach starts the flow of information from customer to you—which is the direction you want. Of course, the responses you generate allow you to learn more about them and thereby create additional layers of comfort.

Open or Closed? Hold the Interrogation, Please

There is an art to creating, building, and eventually asking effective retail customer questions. Just as a surgeon or a sculptor has different tools based on different objectives, so you have different questioning tools and tactics to consider based on the situation you face.

There are two broad, separate categories of questioning: open and closed. Let's take a look at closed-ended questions first. Typically, they will begin with the following words: *can, will, does, do, have, could, would, should.*

When I think of the classic police drama where the suspect is under the bright lights in the interrogation room, I hear these kinds of questions being asked. They always seem to lead to quick, one or two-word responses: *yes, no, don't recall, don't know, not sure.* This dialogue is not very comfortable at all, is it? And it doesn't elicit a lot of information. It's exhausting for both sides. It escalates the pressure. The moral: Don't be an interrogator. Use closed-ended questions sparingly.

One way to avoid the appearance of interrogating is to mix the questions with stories, often using the third-party technique. This is meant to keep the prospect comfortable, disarmed, and able to communicate more easily.

"Customers often ask us about which of these styles is more well suited for everyday wear and which can be worn for business casual when needed. Can you tell me if that might be the case here, and which of these are more relevant to you?"

Open questions will lead to more listening with your prospect while allowing them the opportunity to elaborate, open up and share. Remember: The more they talk, the more we learn. The more they talk, the more they begin to like you. The more they talk, the more they feel heard. Trust goes up. Comfort goes up. So do sales.

Open questions typically begin with: *who, what, where, when, why, how.*

I Keep Six Honest Serving-Men
by Rudyard Kipling

I keep six honest serving-men
    (They taught me all I knew);
Their names are What and Why and When
    And How and Where and Who.
I send them over land and sea,
    I send them east and west;
But after they have worked for me,
    I give them all a rest.

I let them rest from nine till five,
    For I am busy then,
As well as breakfast, lunch, and tea,
    For they are hungry men.
But different folk have different views;
    I know a person small—
She keeps ten million serving-men,
    Who get no rest at all!
She sends 'em abroad on her own affairs,
    From the second she opens her eyes—

One million Hows, two million Wheres,
And seven million Whys!

These six amazing little words can open up our world, one great question at a time.

THE TOOLBOX

Let's now open the retail sales professional's questioning toolbox. Your main tools are:

- The questioning palette
- The reverse
- The amateur curve
- Assumptive questions
- Third-party stories

Why the need for a toolbox?

- To learn more about your prospect and what they really need help with.
- To avoid telling and to do more selling based on what you are discovering.
- To avoid unpaid consulting.

Unpaid consulting happens when the salesperson becomes the expert and tells their prospect everything (and then some). Then, the customer leaves without buying. I was often guilty of this crime in my early years as a retail jeweler. I took great pride in the extensive education I had received about diamonds, gems, precious metals, and fine watches. To further that education, I had attended the Gemological Institute of America and eventually became GIA-certified in diamonds and diamond grading. Eventually, I became, by GIA standards, an official expert. But, as it turned out, I was not yet an expert at building relationships with customers that resulted in purchases, repeat purchases, and referrals.

I quickly learned that I was making plenty of mistakes when it came to my interviewing technique. I was so impressed with this tremendous amount of newly learned scientific data, history, statistics, facts, and information I had mastered that I got my priorities all wrong. When dealing with customers, my initial goal (not a good one) was to demonstrate how knowledgeable and experienced I was. I thought that by telling rather than selling, I could lead them to the belief that I was the best one they could possibly choose to deal with, based on my superior expertise.

It sounded something like this:

Me: "Hi, welcome to our store. Is there anything I can show you?"

Customer: "We are looking for engagement rings."

Me: "OK, great. Congratulations. Have you done any research so far?"

Customer: "No. We are just getting started. Can you tell us why there is such a wide range of pricing of diamonds?"

Me: "I would be happy to. First of all, you should learn all about the four C's, which include color, clarity, cut, and carat. Color means..."

And on. And on. The lecture had officially begun. Students, take your seats, please.

I was chomping at the bit to provide each customer with valuable information that I believed would ultimately help them learn all about what I was selling. After all, I was the expert. They could learn so much from me. Often, they did. But after they had learned everything they wanted to learn from me, they would walk right out the door.

It sounded like this:

Customer: "Thank you. You have been very helpful. Thanks for providing such great information. It sounds as if you have a lot of experience and expertise. Can you tell me the information about this diamond? What are the exact specifications? How much is it, anyway?"

Me: [I would give my price and then...]

Customer: "Thanks. We are going to think about it. This is a big decision, and we should really do some additional research. Do you have a card?"

I delivered vast amounts of unpaid consulting. I didn't realize it, but I had entered the world of showrooming. The prospect makes the decision to explore purchasing something. They proceed to shop around, kick the tires, ask a lot of questions, and get an incredible amount of information from nice salespeople like me whose goal is to provide expert information. They then decide to buy elsewhere, whether at another store or online. But along the way, they get a really good education. For free.

The antidote to the free-consulting trap is actually surprisingly simple: Use your toolkit.

Tool #1: The Questioning Palette

Start thinking of yourself as an artist in front of a canvas. Think of your job as painting a picture, based on the information you get from your customer.

What are you trying to paint a picture of? A solution; something that fills the gap between where the customer is right now and what their desired outcome is. Think of each question as a brushstroke that gets you closer to understanding what your customer really, truly wants to fill that gap with—without sounding too "salesy." In order to paint that picture, you want to work in a certain order. You want to start painting with the broad strokes first, the strokes that fill in the background. Only then can you move into the detail work, the narrow strokes that go in the foreground of the picture.

The problem most retail salespeople have—the problem I used to have—is trying to paint with that narrow brush first. I'll give you an example of what I mean. Someone might walk into my store and explain that she is looking for a Cartier watch for her husband's birthday. I'd immediately say, "Sure,

I can help you with that. Would he prefer quartz movement or automatic?"

How in the world is she supposed to know? That's what I call a "narrow-brush" question. These overwhelm people. Like most customers, she probably does not walk in knowing that quartz movement means battery-powered and automatic means self-winding. (And no, this is no time to start lecturing her about the difference.) Before I start pulling out the narrow, detail-focused questions, I need to paint with a much broader brush. Then, I can fill in the background in my painting of the solution that's going to help her pick out the perfect gift.

For instance, I might say:

> "Sure—I can help you with that. Is it OK if I take a couple of minutes to ask you a few questions about your husband, so we get an idea of the kind of watch that would be the best choice for him?" (Note that this is my up-front agreement.)

> "Is this something he's likely to be wearing at work? What does he do for a living?"

> "Would you say he's a sports-focused person? Is this something he'd expect to wear while hiking or running, for instance?"

And so on. These are what I call "four-inch wide brush questions." They help you fill in the background—and get the broad outlines of the solution you're both looking for. You want to be sure to paint this picture together. It's a collaborative effort. That means that, as you choose the various "colors" from your questioning palette, you always want to start with the broad brushstrokes first, and then move into the more detailed strokes once you both agree on what the background looks like. If you do it the other way around, you add stress to the relationship and you overwhelm people.

TOOL #2: THE REVERSE

Reversing is simply answering a question with another question. The goal here is to discover any unspoken questions behind the question that has just been asked. Very often, there is something unspoken behind a retail customer's question.

For instance, consider the customer who asked you: "Just how big is your store network?" At this stage, you haven't learned anything of consequence yet about why she has walked into the store. Does it really make sense to say, "We have eighteen stores in the tristate region"? Probably not. You don't know why she's asking this. Is she concerned about service? Returns? A gift that she wants someone to be able to pick up at another store? You have no idea. So instead of simply providing the information, you say something like, "That's an interesting question about our store network. Why do you ask?"

Congratulations. You have avoided the "expert" trap, forwarded the conversation, and supported a true dialogue.

You can also reverse by asking questions like:

- "You are telling me that because...?"
- "OK, but that means what?"

- "And...?"
- "Such as...?"

There are a couple of important guidelines to bear in mind when it comes to reversing. First, only reverse at relevant or appropriate times. Some questions the customer poses are good opportunities for reversal, and others aren't. You need to be aware enough to spot the difference. If they ask you where the bathroom is or what time it is, don't say, "Interesting question—what makes you ask that?"

In addition, reverse with a purpose. Early in the discussion, your purpose will be to identify what is really going on in the customer's world, what brought them into the store, and whether there is a gap between where they are right now and where they want to be that you can help to close. This is where making a habit of reversing can make a huge difference. Every time a prospect asks a question, ask yourself, "Do I really know why this person just asked that question?" Usually, you won't. Instead of succumbing to the knee-jerk reaction of instantly answering the question that's been posed (which is something the educational system has trained Americans to do since childhood), you can take the adult approach of posing a question of your own so that you can find out what's driving the inquiry.

It's also important to use a softening statement. That's what the phrase, "That's an interesting question," was—a softening statement. It took a bit of the edge off. Quickly reversing a question without a softening statement can damage rapport. Other softening phrases include, "Hmm," and "I see."

Last but not least, know when to reverse again to get to the real situation or issue. My experience is that it often takes three (varied) reverses, executed tactfully and respectfully, to get a customer to open up about what's actually happening in their world.

Tool #3: The Amateur Curve (or Dummy Curve)

Product knowledge used at the wrong time can be dangerous. Too many retail salespeople, as we have seen, are out to prove their bona fides as an expert. That's not a great objective. In the retail world, it usually makes a lot more strategic sense to approach discussions with customers with the simple curiosity of the amateur. Here's a cautionary tale[*] that illustrates that point.

Once upon a time, there was a young man named Omar who got out of school and got a job as a salesman at one of the "big box" stores. Omar worked in the air conditioner and heater department.

On his first day on the job, an elderly woman walked up to Omar and said, "Can you help me with picking out one of these heaters?"

Understand that at this stage, Omar didn't even know where the heaters were. But he said, "Well, follow me, and we'll find the right one for you."

---

[*] Source: *You Can't Teach a Kid to Ride a Bike at a Seminar,* David Sandler.

Omar wandered the floor, leading the customer. Eventually they came to the spot in the store where the heaters were. They talked about what the customer needed, and Omar asked a lot of good questions. His customer had questions, too. Omar mostly didn't know the answers. In order to give her an answer, he had to pull down a box and read from the outside of it to give her the information she needed. After about ten minutes, they figured it all out. She picked out a model. She was happy! They walked up to the front of the store, when she asked, "Hey, how much am I paying for this?"

Omar shrugged his shoulders and said, "You know what? I'm not sure. Let's figure it out together." He tracked down a catalogue and got the current price. She was happy with it. Then she asked him to show her the checkout aisle. He walked her over to it, carrying the unit, and put the purchase on the little conveyor belt for her. She thanked him for all his help. He said, "You're welcome!" And walked away.

Before she left the store, the customer pulled a manager aside, pointed at Omar, smiled, and said, "That young man is a wonderful salesperson."

A couple of months later, the company sent Omar off to heater school. They taught him all about heaters. Fast forward three more months, when senior management took a look at sales in Omar's heater department. They see the strangest thing. Heater sales were actually down in the months since Omar got all his product training.

The problem was Omar now knew too much. He was an

expert. He talked too much about himself and his product. He wasn't as approachable. He wasn't as disarming. He wasn't as good at listening as he had been on his very first day on the job.

In order to get his sales totals back up to where they had been, Omar had to learn to ask the same kinds of "dummy" questions he had asked on day one. He had to learn how to show the same kind of authentic interest in solving problems side-by-side with the customer that he'd shown before he became an expert. That progression back to good questioning, even if it means pretending you don't know something when you really do, is called the Dummy Curve. (In my training sessions with retail salespeople, I call this technique, which was developed by David Sandler, the "Amateur Curve." Either label works.)

The Dummy Curve

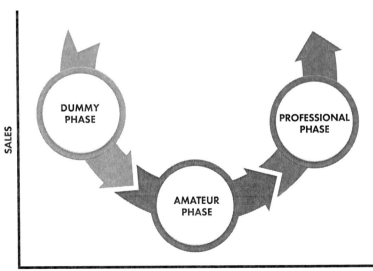

Sometimes it's OK to be a dummy on purpose, to act like an amateur, because that's what disarms the prospect. It's OK to know your product. Just don't feel that you have to share your product knowledge all the time. Be ready to ask the question a dummy would.

The professional salesperson does what they
do as a dummy—on purpose.[*]

One of my clients is a nutritional supplements company, selling to retail stores all over the country. I met several of their talented and highly educated product trainers, people who worked with the sales representatives supposedly to give them all of the data needed to explain the key differences between their products and those of their competitors. Actually, their goal was to educate the retail salespeople to help them sell more of their products by means of product education. They spent a lot of time and energy helping salespeople learn the proper way to explain a given product in minute detail, with the aim of giving each salesperson the ability to sound knowledgeable about the product and ultimately, in the opinion of management, effective.

An interesting thing happened. After the product training, these salespeople felt the need to explain everything

---

* Paraphrased from David Sandler.

in elaborate detail to their customers. Not only that, they stopped asking key questions or trying to learn about their prospect's own reasons for coming into the store in the first place. Sales declined. Why? That's telling, not selling.

Many, many people in retail sales have spent long hours learning about their products or services. They learn all the technical details and all the specifications. They learn all about the pricing and the warranties and the service plans. They learn where specific items are imported from, and what the annual marketing and advertising program looks like. Lots of time, money, attention, and effort goes into this kind of training—typically, far more than goes into retail sales process training. There are plenty of business leaders who appear to believe that product training is the single most effective driver of business. Tell the customer all about the product and give them an education, and they will be a more informed buyer and then buy from you, right?

Wrong.

In retail selling, smart is all too often dumb—and dumb is sometimes a whole lot smarter than you may think. What does proving yourself to be the expert actually accomplish? That old saying is true: People do not care how much you know until they know how much you care—about them.

By the way, this principle holds true in any situation where you are out to prove how much you know, not just in discussions about product and service features. Here's an example of someone playing the expert card—disastrously—in a discussion about pricing.

> **Customer:** "There are online stores that offer this same product for a lot less."

> **Salesperson:** "Really? Which store is that?" (Subtext: "I bet you're wrong," or "I bet I know the online stores better than you do.")

Or:

> **Salesperson:** "Really? Have you checked their warranty?" (Subtext: "If you knew what I know, you'd understand that the true price is actually a lot higher.")

This is questioning designed to prove how smart the salesperson is, how right they are, how much more they know than the customer does. Customers hate it. This kind of questioning literally causes people to leave the store.

Now consider the same statement from the customer, followed by a dummy questioning sequence that's designed to help them reach the relevant conclusions themselves.

> **Customer:** "There are online stores that offer this same product for a lot less."

> **Salesperson:** "I appreciate you letting me know. Could you help me with something—when you say expensive, could you help me understand more of what you mean?"

Customer: "They are selling the same item for less money than you."

Salesperson: "That sounds important to you. Can I ask you a question?"

Customer: "Sure."

Salesperson: "Is your decision to buy this item based on price and price only?"

Customer: "Well, not entirely."

Salesperson: "OK. Can you help me understand what else might be important to you?"

Customer: "Well, service would also be important. In case something needs to be taken care of."

Salesperson: "I appreciate you telling me that. My assumption then is that all aspects of service, delivery, and warranty are exactly the same online as what we are offering. Sounds like you may want to work with them. No problem at all." (Note that you are disarming the customer here, letting them discover for themselves that by keeping total control of the purchase decision, it may not be the best decision in the long term.)

Customer: "Well, the website I looked at said they had great customer service."

Salesperson: "OK. Good to know. Do you mind if I ask you something about that?"

Customer: "Sure, go ahead."

Salesperson: "So, when the online retailer told you they would be giving you in-person customer service, what did they tell you about their response time and their warranty?"

Customer: "I'm not sure if they told me. I don't even know if they have a warranty. Why? What does your warranty look like?"

Now you've got a conversation between peers—a collaborative conversation in which you are both painting the picture of what the solution might look like. That's what you want. Notice that it's the exact opposite of proving to the customer how smart you are.

A friend of mine recently shared a story about a prospect who came into my friend's high-end retail showroom. She asked question after question about the specific features, specifications, and other important information needed to finalize a major new purchase for her home. The customer's questions drove the exchange. My friend asked hardly any questions. After my friend demonstrated his total and indisputable product knowledge mastery, the prospect politely asked for his salesperson's business card, for the store hours, and for website information—and then vanished forever.

My friend later discovered that the very same customer was already speaking with two other stores and a consultant.

She was using all the free consulting my friend had offered to pressure another vendor on price.

The moral of the story: If you're looking to differentiate yourself from the competition, do it by playing the dummy. Do it by asking your own questions, even if you think you know the answer, and learning all the information you possibly can about the customer. You can't expect to set yourself apart by simply shoveling product information to the customer.

Tool #4: Assumptive Questions

In the dummy dialogue I shared with you a moment ago, I used this question, which I'd like you to look at once again:

Salesperson: "So, when the online retailer told you they would be giving you in-person customer service, what did they tell you about their response time and their warranty?"

This is what's known as an assumptive question. It assumes a fact that you know or strongly suspect not to be true. In this case, you are building in the assumption that the online retailer gave the customer lots of information about being committed to in-person customer service, about their typical response times, and about the warranty, when in fact you know or strongly suspect that no such conversations took place.

You're asking this question calmly and without sarcasm or provocation for a specific reason: to help the customer reach a personal conclusion about something important that they may have overlooked. You want the customer to think, "Hey, wait a minute, they never said they would give me in-person customer service. They never said anything about a response time. They never talked about their warranty. I don't even know if they offer a warranty." The light bulb goes on!

Assumptive questions are extremely sophisticated dummy questions, posed with the aim of shining a spotlight on a particular advantage that you know for certain that you hold over a specific competitor. Your best bet is to use these kinds of questions after a customer has raised the name of that competitor and has identified something about their offering that you feel could open up an advantage for your store. Assumptive questions should not be used when you don't know whether you hold a clear competitive advantage in a given area. So, for instance, if you don't know that your competitor has a too-restrictive return policy in comparison with yours, you don't want to ask a question like, "When you asked what the return policy was, what did Store X say?"

Tool #5: Third-Party Stories

Third-party stories give you a great opportunity to transition into important questions that will help you highlight the solution that fills the gap between where the retail customer is right now and where they want to be. For instance:

Salesperson: "In my conversations with people who have been looking at family automobiles, I find that many are concerned about safety, and specifically about side-impact airbags. Is that something that's important to you?"

That's a lot more effective and engaging than simply saying, "Are you interested in safety?" Or: "Are you looking for something with side-impact airbags?" Those questions are so abrupt that they are likely to turn many people off.

Here's something else to consider. Have you ever found yourself in a conversation with a prospect and thought you should say something—but didn't? Did you think speaking your mind might jeopardize the sale? This is your gut talking. Third-party stories give you an extremely powerful way to safely act on that gut instinct.

Suppose a customer is pressuring you to reduce the price on a certain item. Rather than simply caving or "digging in," what if you said something like this:

"Fred, I appreciate what you're asking. I have a bit of a problem with that. You see, about 30 days ago, I had a similar situation with a customer. He asked me to reduce the price. I went to my partner and fought hard to get him a lower price and brought that price back to him. Unfortunately, what he did with that price was to go to another store. Let me ask you a rather direct question: Are we in the same situation now?"

Follow your gut instinct, be candid, and use the right tonality, and you can use third-party stories to help customers paint a mental picture of virtually any situation—and then pose a question that cuts right to the heart of the matter.

THE ART OF LISTENING

Hearing is biological. Listening is a choice. Make that choice. Full disclosure: The questioning toolkit I have shared with you in this chapter will be of no use whatsoever if you can't be bothered to actually listen to the answers you receive. The tools only work if you use your questions to facilitate a respectful two-way communication process.

Before I close out this chapter, let me remind you that listening in a retail setting is an art—an art in which highly effective retail salespeople are constantly looking to improve their proficiency. Here are some of the common mistakes they avoid when it comes to listening skills.

1. **Getting hung up on the past.** Don't assume that a customer who has a certain problem is identical to the last customer who had that problem. Be fully present in the current conversation.

2. **Trying to script the conversation ahead of time.** Allow the conversation to flow naturally, based on the input of the other person. Don't fixate on the internal question, "What will I ask next?"—that's what will keep you from paying attention to what's being said right now. Don't make people feel they are being interrogated.

3. **Zoning out.** "Passive listening" happens when you

don't provide support or feedback to the other person in the conversation. It's often a sign of insecurity: if you don't know what to do, you might simply disengage. This may feel like playing it safe, but it's actually a great way to alienate customers.

4. **Trying to score points.** Have you ever had a conversation with someone who obviously couldn't wait to disagree with you, dispute the accuracy of something you've said, or otherwise prove you wrong? How exhausting was that? The problem is, it's a natural human instinct to want to look good. Often people don't even realize when they're trying to score points at someone else's expense. Without meaning to, you can quickly create a toxic dynamic in the conversation. Make a conscious effort to notice when you're doing this, then focus with full attention and zero judgment on the precious present moment that you are sharing with the customer.

SUMMARY

Key points from this chapter:

- Don't deliver free consulting.
- Use the questioning toolkit.
- Start with "broad brush-stroke" questions first.
- Consider reversing the customer's questions by answering with a question of your own.
- Never use questions to prove how smart you are. Be ready to ask the questions a dummy would ask.
- Know when to ask assumptive questions.
- Use third-party stories to introduce important questions.

TWELVE

Are They Willing and Able?

There is a popular and dangerous "drug" many salespeople take when working with an enthusiastic buyer. This is what we refer to as "hopium." Taken too often, the overall effect of this drug is an enduring delusion that someone is both willing be and able to buy when the evidence is clear that that may not be the case.

Many salespeople have had the experience of mistaking hope for facts when dealing with a buyer. They experience what feels like a "moment of truth" with a retail customer. They think to themself, "I think they are giving me buying signs" or "I'm getting a great feeling about this." Maybe they even heard the customer say some encouraging words: "This is beautiful." Or: "I love it." Or: "Just what we have been looking for!" The salesperson thinks: *This is it! The moment when they say, "I'll take it."*

And then they hear, "OK, let me think it over," "What are your store hours?" or "This looks great—we will get back to you." Sometimes they hear, "It is actually more than I was hoping to spend." Even more often, perhaps, the customer will think that but not say it out loud. They'll mutter something that's hard to make out, and simply walk out of the store. The salesperson's heart sinks.

So, what are the takeaways here? The first, I believe, is that professional salespeople need to understand that there is a clear difference between a customer's willingness to buy and that same customer's ability to make that investment or purchase. Lots of people want a Ferrari. Any number of people might want to test drive a Ferrari. Some people who ask to test drive a Ferrari are going to imply that they're able to afford it when they really can't. That's part of the terrain. Again: Not everyone is qualified to be your customer. Whose job is it to find out whether the customer is qualified to buy? Yours!

Another important takeaway is that there are definitely going to be times when you encounter a customer that you know has the money, someone you really think is going to buy, who doesn't buy. They're able, but they're not willing. If you are foolish enough to press the point, if you add pressure and stress to the conversation, they will make it abundantly clear to you that they're not willing. They will push back. The relationship will suffer. Here again, you need to accept that not everyone is qualified to become your customer. It's possible that the idea of filling the gap between where this buyer is right now and where they would like to end up just isn't compelling enough for them to take action right now. Whose job is it to find out whether the individual is actually motivated enough to take action? Yours!

As I said a little earlier in the book, remember the four "SWs": Some will. Some won't. So what? Stop whining!

This brings us to the third important takeaway about "willing and able"—you have more control over these outcomes than you imagine. Anytime you find yourself surprised by a prospect's decision not to buy, all that means is that you didn't get as much good-quality information up front as you could have. When that happens, you need to ask yourself: "What did I miss? What can I learn from this? How can I get a clearer picture about what's really going on?" The answer to that last question, I believe, is always going to be some variation on, "By having a more effective adult-to-adult, peer-to-peer conversation." That means respecting the customer and the relationship. In the end, that's really the only way to figure out what's really going on.

Let me share with you a very common scenario that will illustrate exactly what I mean by a more effective adult-to-adult conversation.

When I worked in retail jewelry, it was quite common for

a gentleman to come into the shop unaccompanied and ask to see, close up, a certain ring that he liked the look of. Of course, most of these men were shopping for engagement rings for the special woman in their life.

So, picture a man of about thirty—we'll call him Anton—approaching the counter and asking me to give him a closer look at a certain ring. I introduce myself, welcome him, get his name, and then engage in a little chitchat about what brings him into the store. I learn that he's about to pop the question. I tell him I'm happy to help out in any way I can. I take out the ring he's asked to examine. I put it on the counter, and he leans in and takes a close look.

Anton loves it. He examines it from every angle. He's pretty certain his intended will love it, too. He asks, "How much is it?"

I tell him the price.

Anton sighs, shakes his head and says, "Hmm. That's a lot of money."

Let's press pause now. There are two major directions the dialogue can go at this point. I call the first direction the amateur direction because it's the way I would have driven the conversation (and lost the sale) back when I was just getting started in retail.

In the amateur direction, I would have instantly assumed full control of the conversation and shut down effective communication between myself and Anton. I would have done that by instantly putting away the ring after Anton said

"Hmm. That's a lot of money," and then saying something like: "Tell you what, let's look at something that might be a little more affordable."

And taking out another ring.

And then wondering why the conversation dies and Anton leaves without making a purchase.

Here's what happened when I went in the amateur direction: I stopped being an ally and started being a control freak. I told Anton what was going to happen next. So now, on top of having to process how much the ring costs, he also has to process being told what to do along with the possibility that I am somehow judging him and taking away his status as an equal partner in the conversation. I don't know that Anton is unable to buy the ring, but I certainly have done my fair share to make sure he isn't willing. I've done that by adding pressure to the conversation. Again: This is what amateurs do.

Suppose I had taken a different approach. Suppose I had taken the professional direction. Suppose that, after Anton had said, "Hmm. That's a lot of money," I had followed his lead about what to do next by saying something like: "I know. Do you want to keep looking at this one, or should we take a look at something else?"

Notice what this does. First and foremost, it keeps the lines of communication open. Second, it allows me to communicate with Anton as a peer—and not as a vaguely judgmental pseudo-parental figure, which is how I was coming off when I went in the amateur direction. Third, it gives Anton a sense of having control over where the conversation is going to go. That's vitally important. This is one of the most important purchases of his life.

I've dealt with this exact scenario hundreds of times. When you don't pressure Anton—when you follow his lead—guess what happens? Very often he finds the money.

Don't take the amateur route. Don't hijack the conversation. Be a professional. Let the customer tell you what they want to do next. Keep the connection alive. That way, they're much more likely to tell you whether they are able to buy and then show you whether they are willing to buy.

SUMMARY

Key points to remember:

- Keep the lines of communication open.
- Communicate as one adult to another.
- Follow the prospect's lead.
- Don't hijack the conversation. Be a professional. Let them tell you about what they want to do next and about their willingness and their ability to buy.

THIRTEEN

Customer
KARE

L ike many retailers, I enjoy sharing stories about repeat customers. These are the people who frequently stop in, seeking help, advice and consultation, and spread the good word about what a great place our store is. In the world of retail jewelry, their visits are often in preparation for upcoming special occasions. It might be a birthday, a wedding, an anniversary, or some other major life event. At my store, we learned to recognize and make the most of these visits. When one of our best customers showed up, either I or a member of my sales staff would ask questions and help the person make the best possible choices. This was (and is) retail selling at its best: an ongoing relationship, based not on a single impulse purchase, but on trust that has been built up over time by means of careful nurturing.

On one of these occasions, Vicki, a great customer of ours, fell in love with a pair of diamond earrings. These had been suggested by our talented salesperson, Kay. The earrings were to be Vicki's present for an upcoming wedding anniversary. Vicki's husband Bryce, a more practical shopper, had not joined her for this visit; he had no idea of the dimensions of the plan being hatched over the counter.

Vicki was concerned that there might be some resistance on Bryce's part to spending the (significant) amount of money that these earrings carried on their price tag. Clearly, it was time for a creative solution.

Kay said, "Vicki, let me make an unusual suggestion." (By the way, that's an extremely powerful word, "suggestion." Once you have nurtured the relationship and established a deep sense of personal trust, the possibilities really are endless. Once you position what you have in mind as a collaborative suggestion that the customer can either follow or decline, you've got a co-conspirator in the making.)

Vicki said, "What's that?"

"Why don't you take the earrings home? Don't pay us quite yet. We know you're good for it. Tonight, when Bryce comes home, put on the earrings. Only. Nothing else. And tomorrow, come back and tell me whether or not he thought buying the earrings was a good idea."

Vicki liked that suggestion. And she followed it to the letter.

The next day, Vicki came back to the store smiling. Sold! She paid the bill. That's how Kay earned credit for an unforgettable "assist" on two happy people celebrating their anniversary.

Why do I tell you this story? I'm certainly not suggesting this approach is right for every situation. What I'm pointing out is that one of the most important aspects of running a successful retail business is understanding the expectations of your buyers—and specifically understanding their expectations of their relationship with you. Vicki trusted us implicitly (and vice versa). She expected to be given creative ideas. That creative approach of Kay's made perfect sense within the context of the relationship that has been built up over a period of years. If Kay had just greeted Vicki for the first time five minutes earlier, that suggestion would not have been wise or appropriate.

There are four different types of customers in a retail business—four sets of customer expectations, with four different strategies required on your part. All four of these groups are important to understand as part of a comprehensive plan to deepen customer relationships over time. All four of these categories can be developed through a well-thought-out marketing and sales plan, leading to an effective overall strategy, solid growth, and a long list of happy customers recommending you and your business to other people.

The four categories are Keep, Attain, Recapture, and Expand—KARE, for short. Let's look at each of them now.

KEEP

Remember: Your very best customer is also your competitor's best prospect.

Your repeat customers, of course, are the ones you should be most eager to keep. They have been pleased with your offerings, with your service, and with the overall buying experience, and as a result they have come back for more. They would happily recommend you to others, should the topic come up in conversation.

These, then, are people who are genuinely loyal to you and your brand. They come to you first as their solutions provider. The main reason they do that, aside from their perception of value, is the presence of personal trust. You have successfully nurtured the relationship. They love you, and you love them. What are you doing to keep your customers happy, engaged, and coming back for more? Now that you have earned a loyal customer, how do you keep them loyal and recommending you to their family and friends? Think creatively—and find ways to create an even better experience.

Now more than ever, it is vital for retail sales professionals to create steadily greater experiences for their most loyal customers. Isn't that what Kay did for Vicki?

Here are some questions and checklist items that will help you see how effective you are in identifying the loyal customers you want to keep and nurturing the ongoing relationship with them:

- Do you track FCE (first customers ever) who shop in your store?
- Do you track how they got to you in the first place? For instance:

  * Advertisement
  * Referral from a friend, colleague, or family member
  * Social media posts
  * Email campaign
  * Walk in (browsing)

- What do you do to invite them in again after the initial visit?
- What do you do to invite them in again after the first purchase?
- What do you really know about them? Special interests, hobbies, or recreational activities?
- How often do you contact them after the first purchase?
- How are you creating a great buying experience for this unique customer?

  * Do you track repeat purchases?
  * Do you have a loyalty program?
  * Do you express authentic personal gratitude to your best customers in a face-to-face setting? For instance: "Henrietta, I don't often get the chance

to show you how much I appreciate the opportunity for us to work together and how much I appreciate you being as supportive of the store as you have. Thank you. It means a lot to us to have you as a customer."

ATTAIN

The customers you want to attain are, of course, those people in your target market who have not yet had the opportunity to do business with you. Setting up an effective attain strategy is the same as setting up a system that delivers a positive initial experience and interaction with your store and its staff, regardless of whether or not that initial experience results in a purchase.

In addition to a great customer experience (which is what this book has been looking at how to deliver), a good marketing plan can create more awareness of you and your specific value proposition: what you do well and how that benefits the customer.

Today, more than ever, a proactive approach to new customer development has to be more than simply unlocking the doors and hoping people enter. It is a combination of marketing, networking, referral generation, and strategic alliances or partnerships.

It's worth noting, too, that many of these attain customers may come to you by means of a referral from a solid keep customer. It's therefore worth asking:

- What does your initial customer experience feel like to a first-time shopper? How do you know?
- How do make first-time shoppers feel welcome in your store?
- What is your marketing plan?
- What is your referral generation process? How effective is it? Do you ask loyal customers directly for referrals to prospects you could attain as customers? (For example: "Jeanne, just out of curiosity, is there anyone in your world you can think of that we could help in the way we've helped you? Great, here's a coupon for 10% off a first-time purchase. Would you feel comfortable passing that along?")

RECAPTURE

This is the group of people who bought from you previously, but who have since fallen off the radar screen. This could be because they simply haven't thought about you for a while or there were times when the customer experience may not have been perfect and they were not completely satisfied. How do you turn that around? What would it take to bring this customer back? What would it take to recapture their business?

The answer lies in a simple concept: engagement.

There's somebody who bought from you months or even years ago and you haven't seen them in a while. This is the person you want to send an email message to, or even mail a personalized handwritten note to, that says, basically, "We miss you! Our new collection just came in, and it made me think of you. Here's a gift certificate for $X off. Come in and see us again." Or even: "I've been thinking about what happened, and I know you didn't get our best when you came into our store last time. Here's a gift certificate for 25% off your next purchase. We want to do right by you."

In order to make such outreach efforts work, it should go without saying that you must maintain and constantly update your customer database. While it makes sense to stay in touch over time with everyone on your list, it also makes sense to identify those customers who have not bought from you in a while and set up special messaging for them.

- What is your plan to change the course of an unpleasant experience and get the customer to return? What do you do to win such customers back?
- Do you ask for contact information from customers and get their permission to update them regularly about what's going on at your store?
- Do you create customized, personal messaging for special situations?
- How often do you engage with your customers and former customers, and by what means? (You should have a plan.)

EXPAND

This, I believe, is the area of retail that requires the greatest skill because it requires nurturing and supporting the relationship before the purchase is actually concluded. This is the customer who has made the decision to buy from you but hasn't yet checked out. Trust has been established. They are prepared to purchase from you. Now that you have done a good job of listening to them, offering your expertise and guidance, the question is, can you help them by offering further suggestions?

I think of these situations as opportunities to expand the relationship, as opposed to thinking of them as "cross-selling" or "upselling" opportunities. Again: People love to buy, yet hate to be sold. Expanding the relationship is all about making it easier for them to buy from you, today, by making suggestions that make sense in the context of the relationship that you've both created.

The key word here is "relationship." Let me ask you a question. What usually happens when someone tries to upsell you? You resist, right? You hear a robotic question or statement along the lines of, "Would you like fries with that?" That's not exactly a great example of relationship building.

But what happens when a retail sales professional succeeds in expanding the relationship to a new level of trust in real time, before the customer pays for the order? Something very different.

It might sound like this:

Salesperson at a men's clothing store: "Well, I have to say, I think you made a great choice. What do you think? Do you feel comfortable with what you're getting?"

Customer: "You know what? I do. I really love that suit. I can't wait to wear it."

Salesperson: "That's great to hear. Hey, can I make a suggestion?"

Customer: "Sure."

Salesperson: "A lot of people are complementing that particular look with navy blue accents like one of these ties. Here, let me show you..."

Notice how different that is than some monotonous, one-size-fits-all upsell. The exchange feels, and is, natural because it's based on what you actually know about the person and on your own sense of what will work best for them. Notice, too, how the salesperson confirms, before trying to add anything on to the sale, that the customer really is happy, and then some, with the purchase they're already committed to making. If they weren't happy, there would be no reason to suggest an additional purchase. Your job is to make sure the customer is completely satisfied with the purchase before the order is rung up. It's your responsibility to make sure they are thrilled with their purchases as they walk out the door. Last but not least, notice that powerful word again: suggestion. You're not pressuring anyone. You're merely making a suggestion.

- How do you confirm that customers are not just

content, but thrilled, with what they're about to purchase from you?

- Once you know for sure that the customer is thrilled, how can you make a suggestion that expands the purchase, and, ultimately, the relationship?
- Is this an opportunity to increase your average sale?
- What add-on products or services would deliver the most value to your customers?

SUMMARY

KARE for your customers—for life!

The beautiful thing about applying this KARE model to the world of retail is that your relationships with your customers can and often do progress through all four categories. Understanding these four different yet frequently interrelated categories of customer expectations will point you toward a much more effective, proactive customer development and retention process—and make it easier for you to create long-term relationships with your very best customers and increase your average sale.

FOURTEEN

The Seven Steps

Now that you have spent a significant amount of time on the specific do's and don'ts of retail selling, let's step back and look at what a detailed "no pressure" retail selling system looks like from beginning to end. There are seven steps to this system.[*]

This seven-step process will help build rapport and trust with prospects, encourage them to open up and share as well as give the real reasons behind their purchase, and allow you to create maximum value as a retail selling professional.

The objective of the process is to help your customer/prospect get to the moment where they decide for themselves,

---

[*] This system is based on the Sandler Submarine.

without any pressure from you, that they have made a decision to purchase, based on the process of mutual discovery.

1. Bonding & Rapport: The Greeting

You welcome the customer and establish a connection; you build credibility by saying something that is seemingly not in your own best interest (such as, "Let's find out if we're a good fit for you; we might not be"). The goal here is to be disarmingly honest.

You strive to understand the person's communication style and the science of DISC. Specifically, you learn to recognize and adapt effectively to each of these different, yet equally important styles or groups:

- **Dominant:** direct, to the point, bottom-line oriented ("Let me see what you have.")
- **Influencer:** engaging, talkative, expressive, animated ("It is so great to meet you. I have some friends that shop here.")
- **Steady Relator:** friendly, trustworthy, easy-going ("Is there something you would suggest for me?")
- **Compliant:** driven by data, numbers, analysis ("I have questions regarding the specifications and product capabilities.")

2. Up-Front Agreement

With an up-front agreement,* you set the agenda for the interaction. This agreement can take many forms and may be revised and repeated as necessary. Establish parameters at the beginning so that you and the prospect/customer are clear with regard to mutual expectations of time, objectives, and potential outcomes.

I've seen retail interactions range from a mere five-minute discussion to a sale all the way to at least an hour or more of engagement. Whatever time you think it may take to learn more about your prospect and their goals, whether immediate or longer term, it is best to get some guidelines as to how long they might expect their interaction with you to take. In some cases, they may not know. Here is an opportunity to guide and coach them through the process by sharing how you work as a retail selling professional, knowing the time guidelines.

Remember, this is a mutual process of discovery. At some point, you will want to discuss:

- **Their agenda and yours.** Yes, you have an agenda, and you need to talk about it. You do have certain rights and responsibilities both sides have to respect in order to help your customer make the best possible decision. You have the right to ask questions to better

---

* As mentioned earlier, this step is known as the Up-Front Contract in classic Sandler terminology.

understand them, their preferences, concerns, and any misinformation they may have received from others.

- **Questions:** Your role as a retail selling professional is to ask questions and learn more before jumping in to find the instant solution or product. Remember, without doing a deep dive of questioning, you may find yourself doing unpaid consulting and potentially miss the mark. Giving a lot of information and educating them without getting anything of equal or greater value is unbalanced.

- **Outcome(s):** What are some likely outcomes at the end of your discussion with your customer? Be ready to talk about these.

I often ask salespeople, "What are the potential outcomes of a retail sale?" They will typically answer getting a *yes* or a *no* as the two most probable alternatives. Salespeople do love a *yes*. Salespeople should also find *no* to be the second-best answer. This is because you avoid the nebulous, uncertain, maybe, think-it-over, type of answers from your prospect/customer. But there are two more possibilities for good outcomes: setting a clear next step (instead of getting a "maybe" response), and learning a lesson from the exchange should things not work out so you can do a better job next time around.

Remember those words from those uncertain customers who wished to reassure the average salesperson? "I'll be back," or "What are your hours?" These would always lead me into the land of hoping, wishing, and assuring myself they really would come back. After all, they were nice people and seemed interested. The real and brutal truth is that although some did return at a later date, most of them never, ever came back.

You can reduce the number of "think-it-overs" by making people feel more comfortable. Simply let them know in your agreement that if there isn't a fit, or if you aren't right for each other, you are going to let them know and would ask for them to do the same in return.

The other option might be that there is a fit between you and your prospect. What is important at this point is to let them know how they may buy from you. For some industries or businesses, there might be a credit application process as a first step. For others, it might mean taking out a credit card and the sale is done. There's no need to overcomplicate the process. Just know when to concisely tell your customer how they may buy from you. In many cases, it is a very simple way: Pay for it. Done.

3. FINDING THE REAL REASONS TO DO BUSINESS

Consistently employing this step* of discovery will be the true differentiator between you and your competition. It involves a mutual discovery process based on the solid questioning techniques outlined in Chapter 11. In short, this step

---

* This step is known as the Pain Step in classic Sandler terminology.

is selling to the gap between where the customer is right now and where they want to go. It is engaging emotion, rather than citing features and benefits. Imagine the joy, excitement, and happiness of a special gift; imagine the concern, fear, and anxiety of a less-than-ideal outcome. These are extremely powerful motivators. They are rooted in human emotion, the ultimate source of the desire to buy.

4. BUDGET/INVESTMENT

At some point you are likely to hear the words: "How much is it?" This can sometimes—not always, but sometimes—lead to an awkward moment.

Many salespeople fall into the trap of explaining the price by launching into an instant monologue about the great value. This only makes them sound like everyone else. You may be asked about discounting or challenged about whether the price you cite is truly "the best price." You can avoid both of these traps by using a bracketing strategy:

"Typically, the people I speak with invest between $X and $Y. Is this somewhere within the ball park of where we need to be?" The addition of a third-party story will help you sound less "salesy" and more credible at the same time. Alternatively, some people suggest showing the customer the most expensive item first and then, based on their reaction, begin the selling process to find the comfort area. Find a strategy that works for you and that you feel comfortable with. The key is to get a sense of your customer, their DISC style, and their reactions, so you can have a productive adult-to-adult conversation.

Here are some key phrases that effective salespeople use when it comes time to discuss money:

"Do you have a budget in mind?"

"Can you share with me in round numbers what that might be?"

"I'm trying to get a gut feel of the amount."

"I'm not going to hold you to it."

For those who might get some pushback with pricing, here is a suggested question:

Salesperson: "Do you mind if I ask you a rather direct question?"

Prospect: "No, I don't mind."

Salesperson: "Is your decision to buy based on price and price only?"

To discuss pricing in a truly grown-up way, you must come to terms with your own money messages that come from your own childhood. My father was an entrepreneur, which meant in his early years of starting his own retail jewelry business he faced many financial struggles. I remember my father coming home after an exhausting day and sitting with us at the dinner table. We children would share our stories of the day, which might have included the latest and greatest new toy or gadget we saw someone else playing with. His curt response would be, "We can't afford that right now."

I started thinking of money as a limited resource, something there was never enough of. In my work with many salespeople, I have learned that this is a very common scenario. Those who had grown up in a home where money was scarce would have a very different money concept than someone who grew up in a home where money was plentiful. Similarly, those who grew up being told, "It is impolite to talk about money," tend to have other challenges when discussing pricing with customers. The moral here is: You must clean up your own head trash or self-limiting beliefs around money (as well as other areas). Finding a coach or mentor can help you make progress in this important area.

My basic suggestion when it comes to pricing is to just give the price, observe the reaction and then follow this simple rule: "Never defend, justify, or explain."*

5. Uncover the Decision-Making Process

Find out in your interaction how they're going to go about making this purchase decision. This is just as important as determining the customer's reason to buy and their budget. As you talk about the decision-making process, be sure to shine a light on the silent decision influencers that exist in

---

*   Source: David Sandler.

the modern buying cycle. These include competing websites, social media platforms, online reviews, and blogs. This is one of the big reasons you have built up rapport and nurtured the relationship up to this point: so that the customer will share with you what their key influencers and major criteria are. Get into the habit of using effective questions to find out more about the way your customer or prospect makes decisions about an intended purchase. Good questions about the buyer's decision-making process include:

"When would you be needing this?"

"What has to happen between now and then?"

"How do you typically make decisions such as this?"

"What is the timeline for when you would like to see this delivered?"

"What kind of information, specifically, are you looking for before you make a final decision?"

"Where should we get that information?"

"How can I help?"

Use these questions to illuminate how your prospect makes decisions. Bear in mind that, in reaching a decision, some people may look for guidance from a spouse, significant other, friend, family member, or even that silent decision maker, the internet. Respect their process. Never put pressure on them.

6. Fulfillment

Based on the information gathered thus far, make a suggestion that fulfills the customer's expectations, stop talking, and see what happens. Many salespeople don't make suggestions. They rush into what they would much rather do: talk at length about their products or services. That's far less effective. And, of course, if there is not yet a clear understanding of the prospect's needs, wants, and concerns, the monologue will backfire spectacularly. Remember: Telling is not as effective as selling.

Make the best suggestions you possibly can. See what the response is.

If the prospect actually feels confident that you, as a sales professional, have helped them make a good decision about their purchase, a decision that they've reached on their own power with a little assistance from you, then they will respond positively to your suggestion and they will buy. If they don't feel you've done that, they won't. It's as simple as that.

7. Post-Sell

Make absolutely certain they are thrilled with their purchase. Thank them for the opportunity of working with them. With their permission, get them on your email list.

For instance:

Salesperson: "Jasmine, first and most importantly I want to thank you for the opportunity you've given us to work together. Please remember that we're here in case you have any questions or concerns whatsoever—our door is open. Secondly, I am hopeful that you are happy with what you got. Are you?"

Customer: "Yes. Very much so."

Salesperson: "Great. One more question. We have customers who ask to be placed on an email list for upcoming promotions and special client and customer appreciation events. If you are OK with providing us with your contact information, we would be happy to include you also. Is that OK?"

Customer: "Sure."

If you've done your job properly up to this point, the person will definitely want to hear from you about these things.

SUMMARY

As you can see, there is a clear process to effective retail selling. This process includes both psychological and behavioral elements because you're creating and supporting a relationship, not just closing a sale. An average salesperson may possess some of these key ingredients; the master has proficiency in all seven areas.

This is an ideal time to examine your own way of selling and make the necessary changes to improve it so that it aligns with what you've learned here.

Commit to the process, not the outcome. Following this simple rule will distinguish you from your competitors, offline and online.

In the Epilogue, I'll share some final thoughts on retail sales success.

EPILOGUE

The insights and strategies I have shared with you in the main section of this book are meant to help you make the transition from being the kind of retail salesperson most of us encounter (a vendor) to being a true retail *champion*—a trusted advisor, a professional. As additional resources, you will find three special champion appendices following this Epilogue. The first is a summary of champion in-store best practices. The second offers recommended champion strategies on engaging with customers over time after they have made an initial purchase. The third offers some thoughts on reducing turnover by improving your hiring and retention process so that your store is staffed by a team of champions. Each of these appendices represents a distillation of literally decades of experience.

Before we close, though, I want to share something very important with you. Success, as you have seen, is a matter not just of technique but of behavior and attitude as well. I know the techniques I have shared with you in these pages are effective. They have worked for me and for many people I have trained. But I also know that just understanding the techniques, just reading about them in a book, is not enough.

If you are serious about becoming a champion—and if you've made it this far in the book I have to believe you are— then I know you will believe me when I tell you that reading is not enough. You need a shift in attitude—and a shift in behavior, as well. You need peer support and ongoing rein- forcement in the fundamentals of success in order to make the kinds of sustainable changes that will allow you and your retail store, whether you are a national retailer, multi-store chain, or independent retailer, to thrive in the Amazon era. You need, in short, to take the next step. I hope you will take that next step by visiting us online at retail.sandler.com and learning more about what Sandler Training has to offer.

I look forward to hearing from you.

Rob Fishman

APPENDIX A

The Retail
Champion's Playbook

R etail champions never stop asking themselves questions about how to improve the customer experience. The answers to these questions generate a unique playbook for your store that sets it apart from competitors.

CHAMPION QUESTIONS FOR OWNERSHIP

- Have you done a visual inspection of your store from the outside looking in, from the perspective of your prospective customer?
- Have you asked yourself how your window/exterior

display will cause a prospective customer to stop in their tracks and decide to come in?

- Is the visual appeal of the store's interior high? Be brutally honest with yourself. What visual first impression does your store's interior deliver when someone walks in? How could that be improved?
- Is there a display near the front of the store that will pull people in?
- Does the interior layout and merchandising plan create a natural traffic flow that makes prospective customers want to walk through your store?
- Does your store's layout and flow avoid bottlenecks?
- Is your store clean?
- Is your store well-organized?
- Appeal to the visual buyer: Is the store's color scheme well planned and attractive?
- Appeal to the auditory buyer: Is there appropriate music?
- Appeal to the kinesthetic buyer: Can prospective customers touch and physically sample merchandise?
- Have your front-line employees been trained to engage with people and initiate good conversations? (Have they read this book?)
- Do your front-line employees have permission to solve problems that arise, up to a certain dollar amount, by giving the customer a gift certificate or other offering?
- Do your front-line employees have permission

to reward loyal repeat customers, up to a certain dollar amount, by giving the customer a coupon or gift certificate?

- Do you have a clear set of standards for employees to follow when customers have a complaint or want to make a return? For instance, do you make it clear to both employees and customers that your store will discuss and authorize exchanges, rather than cash refunds, for returns that meet certain criteria? Helpful hint: Avoid using the word "policy" when describing these processes. The word "policy" sends one and only one message to customers: "We are inflexible."

- Do you have a customer council—a network of loyal customers who can give you regular insights and feedback on what's working in your store (and what isn't) on a mutually convenient schedule?

CHAMPION QUESTIONS FOR FRONT-LINE STAFF

- Do you avoid at all costs saying the words, "Can I help you?" These words instantly bring up the customer's defenses—and keep them up.

- Do you welcome the customer to the store and make the customer feel like an honored guest? One great way to do this is to say, "Hi! Welcome! I'm [name]. And you are...?" Another great way to do this is to say, "Welcome! I'm [name]. Have you been here before?"

- Do you make your best effort to notice and adapt to the customer's DISC style? (See Chapter 10.)
- Do you establish rapport with the customer in a manner that respects the person's DISC style? (See Chapter 10.)
- Do you follow the customer's lead in creating and supporting a zero-pressure conversation?
- Are you striving to make a friend with each customer you greet? When you welcome people to the store, are you making an authentic effort to get to know them as people, not just as customers? This effort is a huge part of what distinguishes your store from online competitors.
- Do you notice and acknowledge friends and family who accompany a customer and introduce yourself to them as well?
- Are you open to conversations about the customer's friends and family? Such exchanges are hallmarks of a long-lasting, mutually beneficial relationship with the customer.
- Do you take the time to learn more about the customer as the conversation proceeds?
- Without interrogating the customer or engaging in any kind of questioning likely to alienate them, do you do your best to connect the purchase being considered to this person's interests, occupation, personal priorities, and so on? For instance: If someone

is shopping for a set of golf clubs, is the set for them? What's their handicap? If a person is shopping for a piece of jewelry for a "special someone"—is it for a special occasion such as an anniversary or a birthday?

- When a customer has a complaint or challenge, do you avoid at all costs citing "policy"?

- When a customer has a complaint or challenge, do you immediately demonstrate empathy? For example: "I'm so sorry to hear that," or "I'm really sorry you had a problem with the product." Note that empathizing with the customer's emotional response is not the same thing as sympathizing with the specifics of the customer's complaint. When you empathize, you are acknowledging that a negative personal experience exists and expressing emotional solidarity with the customer. You are not accepting the details of the customer's version of what happened. Empathy is essential, and it must happen right away.

- When a customer has a complaint or challenge, do you let the person vent without interrupting?

The Retail Champion's Long-Term Engagement Strategy

etail champions don't just do a great job of connecting with customers while they are face-to-face. They set up a long-term engagement strategy for after the customer leaves the store—and they give customers plenty of reasons to keep coming back.

Such a strategy begins with an effective dialogue allowing the customer to opt in to a mailing list, using MailChimp or a similar piece of software. The list can be used to keep customers informed about upcoming promotions, special offers, new product arrivals, and customer appreciation activities. The champion strategy then continues with an ongoing, continuously updated schedule of events tailored to both the interests of the ideal customer and the ongoing marketing strategy of the store.

CHAMPION EMAIL OPT-IN PROCESS

Salesperson: "Jack, first and most important, I want to thank you for the opportunity you've given us to work together. Please remember that we're here in case you have any questions or concerns whatsoever—our door is open. Second, I am hopeful that you are happy with what you got. Are you?"

Customer: "Yes. Very much so."

Salesperson: "Great. One more question. We have customers who ask to be placed on an email list for upcoming events and special client and customer appreciation events. If you are OK with providing us with your contact information, we would happy to include you also. Will that work for you?"

Customer: "Sure."

You can easily adapt the above discussion to a list that includes text updates via the person's smartphone or some other form of convenient contact. If you've engaged effectively with the customer up to this point, listened carefully, and guided them through the wilderness toward a purchase decision that really does make sense, rest assured that this person will want to stay in touch.

Once you've gotten the person's contact information, it's a matter of sending a properly spaced sequence of concise "drip" messages about upcoming events in your store. Don't bombard your list. Don't go for long periods of radio silence, either. Aim for a consistent pattern of messaging over time. Once a week or once every two weeks are good initial places to start. Measure the open response rate for your messages and adapt your schedule accordingly, making sure never to deluge customers with too many emails in too short a period of time.

Be sure to focus on valuable content in your marketing mix— information that is helpful to your customer, i.e., "ways to keep your new car running well and reduce repair costs," or "the best tips for taking care of your new automatic watch." Consider giving valuable support and information before you ask the reader to take action on a promotion, sale, or new collection.

Give customers at least 72 hours advance notice of all events; a message ten days before the event and then three days before the event, requesting RSVPs in all messaging, is a good model to follow. Send a welcome message as the first digital contact once someone joins your mailing list. Make sure your messages sound like one human being speaking in a relaxed, authentic way to another. That's what motivates customers to keep engaging with your content—and returning to your store. Promptly honor all drop requests, or set up your email program to do it automatically when people opt out.

CHAMPION IN-STORE EVENTS PROCESS

The only real limits here to creative and engaging events are your knowledge of your customers' interests and your own imagination. A brief sampling of ideas that can and have piqued customer interest and resulted in successful in-store events, more foot traffic, and more sales appears below.

- **Free inspection/maintenance assessment.** For instance, in our jewelry store, we would send out a message advising that the customer's purchase price included a free one-year inspection of the item by a qualified jeweler and advice on how best to keep the item looking and feeling new. This can be adapted to any number of product areas.

- **New collection/model has come in.** Update customers about new product offerings that are relevant to their world. The more customized this offer is, the more effective it is likely to be. You may want to emphasize a special discount available only to returning customers.

- **Trunk show.** This is an invitation-only sales event at which a particular designer or company presents selected merchandise to potential customers. It is typically held in a jewelry shop, a clothes shop, or the clothing or jewelry department of a large store. Think personalized fashion show. This is typically an upscale event. Serve champagne—make it fun!

- **Charity event.** At our jewelry store, we did an event to benefit the American Cancer Society; we donated 20% of each purchase to the society and promoted the evening via a local radio station. It was a huge success.

- **Cigar/wine night.** If cigar or wine aficionados happen to be your target market—and in many upscale retail settings they are—give them a special reason to come into your store. Variations on this high-end relationship-building event include cheese and wine pairings, classical music nights, and any type of gourmet food-tasting events.

- **Customized personal events.** One of the most memorable events we ever held at our jewelry store was a surprise event involving a couple. The gentleman proposed to his future wife in our store. We provided the music (yours truly was at the grand piano in the middle of the store) and the food, based on a special arrangement with the gentleman, who was a long-term customer of ours. Family members were hiding in the back until he proposed and the piano music started. Talk about an event to remember! You wouldn't be able to promote a specific event like this via your digital mailing list, of course, but you would certainly be able to make it clear that it's a special service you provide—and that the guests of honor might love to invite family and friends.

All of these events, and their best variations, create a sense of being special, of being part of the in-crowd, of being a member of a special club or tribe—just by shopping at your store. That's the feeling you want to create. That's the whole purpose of engaging over the long term. Don't make it about a single event. Make it about belonging to a unique group, about feeling special, today and for the foreseeable future.

(Of course, you can adapt this event-driven strategy to communications that take place on your website, on Facebook, on Twitter, on Instagram, and indeed on any communication platform.)

Last, But Not Least

In addition to maintaining and regularly updating your digital mailing list, you should also strongly consider sending brief handwritten thank-you notes to your best customers. Very few retailers do this, so it's a great way to stand out from the crowd and leave a long-lasting positive impression. Nothing beats, in my opinion, the sincere appreciation demonstrated in a handwritten note of thanks. (Of course, the note can also contain additional information unique to your relationship with a specific customer.)

Keeping an eye on technology: While staying with tried and true methods of showing appreciation, it is equally important to adapt to the ever-changing world and how technology has evolved, especially in the retail world. Successful retailers and their marketing departments are embracing these changes to their (and their customers') benefit. Wish lists creation, photos, text reminders, and interactive websites are examples of making the store visit even more special.

APPENDIX C

On Turnover, Hiring, and Retention

We hear two common complaints from virtually all of the many retail owners and managers we work with: Employee turnover is too high, and it's nearly impossible to find good people. Very often, in fact, these owners and managers start their discussions about what needs to happen next in their stores with these two complaints—and don't feel much inclined to move the conversation forward from there.

Do those two complaints arise consistently in your own world? Do you find yourself saying these things to yourself, or variations on them? If so, this part of the book is here to help you challenge that kind of thinking and to ask you to consider the possibility that you may be working the wrong end of the problem. Our experience is that stores in which turnover is too high and where good people don't stick around are stores where leadership has not set the vision nor invested in people. You invest in inventory; you invest in equipment; you invest in the retail space customers experience; you probably invest in your store's online presence. All of these are important investments, to be sure. But equally critical are your investments in time, attention, energy, training, and dollars when it comes to the human beings who interact face-to-face with your customers.

The following questions will help you prioritize your people investments, not just financially, but in every other aspect of your retail operation. If you consider these questions closely and act on their honest answers, you will find that your turnover problem—your problem of not being able to find and hold onto quality people—will be a thing of the past.

- **Have you set and communicated your company's vision—its reason for existing?** Do employees know why you open your store's doors every day? Do you? Does your personal vision align with your organizational vision? A great example of a retail vision statement comes from Nordstrom: "Nordstrom's Commitment: In store or online, whenever new opportunities arise, Nordstrom works relentlessly to give customers the most compelling shopping experience possible. The one constant? John W. Nordstrom's founding philosophy: offer the customer the best possible service, selection, quality, and value." Don't recycle Nordstrom's vision—identify yours, make sure it matches up with your personal vision, and communicate it to everyone in your organization.

- **Do you have a clear hiring process?** Does it follow the SEARCH model (skills, experience, attitude, results, cognitive skills, habits) outlined below? Gut instinct is not enough when it comes to hiring.
- **When interviewing for the ideal retail salesperson, do you screen for *skills*?** This does not mean you need to only identify people who have worked with a similar product/service or in a similar field; to the contrary, it often means looking for people who have demonstrated people skills that clearly show up in your interview discussions. For instance:

  * Are they comfortable talking about money?
  * Do they put people at ease? (A familiarity with the DISC behavioral model is often an integral part of this skill.)
  * Are they able to create and sustain rapport easily with people they meet for the first time?
  * Are they comfortable asking questions?
  * Do they listen to the answers they receive and adjust course in the conversation?

* Do they have an overall concern for other people, and try to help them solve problems?

* Do they see things from the customer perspective?

• **When interviewing for the ideal retail salesperson, do you screen for *experience*?** This does not mean you need to only identify people who have worked in retail. Look beyond retail. Don't fall into the trap of hiring based on the person's level of product knowledge; some people who have extensive product knowledge are ill suited to customer-facing sales positions. You can train the product knowledge—but you can't train for being comfortable with customers. Look for relevant people experience overlaps in terms of the person's entire background; consider the entirety of the candidate's professional and volunteer experience. Ask yourself:

* Does this person's work experience suggest a fit with your store?

* Does this person's professional experience include high levels of customer contact?

* Has this person interacted with a wide variety of people and knowledge levels?

* How close does this person's professional background match up with your store's working environment? For instance: if their experience suggests a pattern of being rewarded for slow and methodical

progress on a complex project, in an isolated environment, but your store's working environment is fast-paced and built around creating face-to-face wins in the short term for a steady stream of walk-in customers, that may not be a great fit.

- **When interviewing for the ideal retail salesperson, do you screen for *attitude*?** This is vitally important.

  * Does this person have an optimistic outlook?
  * Are they a self-starter?
  * Do they see adversity as a challenge?
  * If this person has a problem, do they take it to the person who can solve it or talk behind that person's back?
  * Does this applicant buy into your vision and your store's culture?

- **When interviewing for the ideal retail salesperson, do you screen for *results*?** In other words:

  * Does this person have a track record that points toward commitments honored, problems solved, and relationships created and sustained?
  * How do you know?
  * Are the person's references strong? Have you spoken to them personally?

- **When interviewing for the ideal retail salesperson, do you screen for *cognitive skill*?** For instance:

- Can the person follow a clearly documented sales process?
- Do they understand the importance of relationship building in selling?
- Are they adept at problem solving, and can they come up with creative solutions for an individual buyer?

- **When interviewing for the ideal retail salesperson, do you screen for *habits*?** Ask yourself:

  - Do the person's actions match up with their talk?
  - How do you know?
  - Does the person take personal responsibility for oversights and errors and create action plans for fixing them?
  - Is the person proactive?
  - Is the person punctual?
  - Is the person groomed and dressed according to the brand, look, and feel of your store?

- **Do you have a playbook for new employees—a written collection of best practices they can follow right away?** This should be part of your onboarding process.

- **Do you invest in your employee's ongoing personal and professional development?**

* Have you trained your people in specific best practices?
* Have you reinforced that training appropriately?
* Do you have regular one-on-one coaching meetings with your people?

- **Have you set up a team bonus plan?** My experience is that individual bonus plans undercut team spirit in the retail environment. Set up a clear financial incentive based on the team achieving an aggressive income goal within a clear, relatively brief, period of time.
- **Have your employees read this book?** Make sure they do!

Look for these other books on shop.sandler.com:

SALES SERIES
Asking Questions the Sandler Way
Bootstrap Selling the Sandler Way
Call Center Success the Sandler Way
Digital Prospecting
The Contrarian Salesperson
LinkedIn the Sandler Way
Prospect the Sandler Way
Sandler Enterprise Selling
The Sandler Rules
The Unapologetic Saleswoman
Why People Buy
You Can't Teach a Kid to Ride a Bike at a Seminar

MANAGEMENT SERIES
Change the Sandler Way
Customer Service the Sandler Way
Lead When You Dance
Motivational Management the Sandler Way
The Right Hire
The Road to Excellence
The Sales Coach's Playbook
The Sandler Rules for Sales Leaders
The Success Cadence
Transforming Leaders the Sandler Way
Winning from Failing

MOTIVATIONAL SERIES
Accountability the Sandler Way
From the Board Room to the Living Room
Sandler Success Principles
Succeed the Sandler Way

INDUSTRY SERIES
Making Channel Sales Work
Patient Care the Sandler Way
Selling in Manufacturing and Logistics
Selling Professional Services the Sandler Way
Selling to Homeowners the Sandler Way
Selling Technology the Sandler Way

ACHIEVE SALES LEADERSHIP EXCELLENCE WITH

BUILD A BULLETPROOF BUSINESS

A step-by-step guide to:

- **Recruiting and Hiring**: Shed light on leadership blindspots so you and your team can reach your goals.
- **Mentoring and Coaching**: Restructure your leadership processes for long-lasting, positive effects on your business.
- **Goal Setting and Culture**: Identify the bottlenecks that are holding you and your team back from success.

ONLINE EDUCATION DESIGNED FOR QUICK RESULTS
13 modules
13 videos
Blindspots survey
Management and Leadership forum

Designed for managers who are:

- Ready to identify and overcome common leadership blindspots that prevent them and their team from reaching their goals.
- Ready to rethink their current leadership style in exchange for long-lasting, positive effects on their business.
- Currently struggling with lack-luster results based on their existing hiring, onboarding, and coaching methodology.

ENROLL TODAY AT

reports.sandler.com/build-a-bulletproof-business/